Through
Santa's Eyes

Through Santa's Eyes

Be Less Selfish
Be More Elfish

COZ GREEN

Published by North Pole Publishing LLC

Book cover design by Coz Green and Spike Spiegel
Book interior design by Francine Platt, Eden Graphics, Inc.

Photo Credits:
Pictures with Santa and Rory – Megan Rusin
Pictures at the Back of Book – Ben Green

Paperback ISBN 979-8-218-96672-0
eBook ISBN 979-8-218-96702-4
Audiobook ISBN 979-8-218-96703-1

Library of Congress Control Number: 2023920492

First Edition
Manufactured in the United States of America
10 9 8 7 6 5 4 3 2 1

Additional copies of this book are available for bulk purchases.
North Pole Publishing LLC
2900 South 400 West
Salt Lake City, UT 84115
801-244-6300

Email: love@throughsantaseyes.com
Website: ThroughSantasEyes.com

Dedicated to Megan and Ben

Santa and Rory

CONTENTS

Letter to You

My dear friend:

Thank you for reading my book. It is based on my personal experiences since 1999 when I received the call and began seeing the world through Santa's eyes.

Through Santa's Eyes is more than a Christmas book. It's a movement to unite countries, communities, and families around the central message of love and service.

Santa Claus is much more than a character we conjure up during the holiday season; he is a symbol of goodness, hope, love, and giving. These values have the power to change our world for the better. Santa Claus has the power to remind all of us what the true meaning of Christmas is and lead us to Jesus Christ; He is the reason for the season.

We need more peace on earth and good will toward men. We need it more than ever before. We live in an age where up is down, and down is up; where wrong is right, and right is wrong. Jimi Hendrix said, "When the power of love overcomes the love of power, the world will know peace." The power of love can heal broken hearts, mend relationships, and save lives. There is an opposing force that seeks to divide us. It preys on our selfishness, creating a world full of dissonance and chaos.

The simple **"Be Less Selfish, Be More Elfish"** message can change the world. Imagine the world we would live in if people were less focused on instantly gratifying themselves, and lived a life centered on loving God, their families, neighbors, and strangers.

In my life, I have received three distinct "Field of Dreams" moments and was prompted to do something remarkably unique. In the winter of 1999, I was directed to become Santa Claus. My daughter Megan was five years old, and my son Ben was almost eighteen months old. I had a choice: either hide my activities as Santa Claus from my children or be out in the open and make them an active part of it; I chose for Megan and Ben to be involved in every detail.

In chapter one, Megan discovers the letter from Santa Claus and all of his gear. This story is completely true; it is exactly how I staged the scene and created the magic of Santa Claus with my children.

In chapter two, I receive a letter from Santa Claus giving me instructions and coaching. This part of the story is fictionalized and is a synthesis of the lessons I have learned through Santa's eyes since 1999. You could say that the Santa of today is writing a letter to the rookie Santa back then. My dialogue with Santa Claus is also for storytelling purposes and to add a unique dimension to the story. Surrender to the story and enjoy it.

The Christmas stories I share with you are based on actual events I've witnessed. I've couched these stories in the first-person narrative as Santa Claus traveling from the North Pole so you can share these stories with children of all ages. I will release a version of these stories as an illustrated children's book in the future.

I believe the values, traits, and personality of Santa Claus and the spirit he embodies can reside in each one of us. It's a conscious choice. The Christmas Spirit does not need to be something we trod out once a year, but an energy, a frequency we can choose to be in resonance with each day of the year.

It is my mission to spread the **"Be More Elfish"** message to every corner of the world and affect millions of lives. I know this is a big, hairy audacious goal. Through my words and actions, I hope to inspire others to live a life guided by the values Santa Claus embodies. For it is only through love and service that we can unite as a people and create a world that is truly worth living in.

I challenge you to join our movement to **"Be Less Selfish and Be More Elfish."** I'm filled with a deep sense of gratitude for this cause and the lessons I have learned by seeing the world through Santa's eyes.

With much love,

Coz

P.S. I would like to hear from you. Email me at love@ThroughSantasEyes.com and share your experiences with this book and sharing the **"Be More Elfish"** message. Also, share your personal Santa Claus experiences.

P.S.S. To receive a **"Be More Elfish"** wristband, go to www.ThroughSantasEyes.com and share your shipping address. I will send you one free.

～ 1 ～

The Calling

The greatest thing is not to believe in Santa Claus;
it is to be Santa Claus.

– PAT BOONE

I HAD EVERYTHING; then one night, I lost it all as my entire world collapsed around me. During those dark nights of my soul, my life was changed forever when I was given the miraculous gift of seeing the world through Santa's eyes.

Truly, my life back then was full of everything I ever wanted. I had a beautiful wife and two amazing children. We were living in a new home, in a nice neighborhood, surrounded by good neighbors. I was a blessed man. Being a good husband and father means everything to me. I dreamed as a young boy growing up that someday I would have my own big family with an abundance of love and happiness in our home.

Before I tell you my story of how I became Santa Claus, let me take you back a few years and set the stage for why I wanted my own family full of love and happiness.

I'm the youngest of three children. My brother Kelvin is five years older than me, and my sister Paulanne is twenty months older. The three of us are very different from each other. My brother was a Sterling Scholar, and it seemed, growing up, that everything he did was perfect. My sister was quiet and reserved. I, on the other hand, didn't seem to fit in.

I was small and lean. I was shy and couldn't lead silent prayer in a phone booth. I learned to keep my mouth shut for fear of getting the wooden spatula or the belt. But I also had an imagination, a sense of wonder and adventure, and a lot of big dreams.

My brother and sister were more like my dad, Paul. He was quiet and unassuming; he just went to work. He didn't have any hobbies or any outside interests except for being a clerk in our local church. My mother Delpha was the opposite of my dad. She was loud, fun, creative, entrepreneurial, and extremely service-oriented.

Our home was less than harmonious. My mom was strong-willed and very independent. When she became angry and frustrated, she became a yeller. She definitely didn't have a quiet, inside voice. When she and my dad would fight, I'm confident the neighbors two blocks away heard every syllable of the argument. My mom threw things and slammed doors. When she'd had enough, she would head out the back door, slam it twice for dramatic effect, belt out a scream, and then jump in our old GMC pickup truck and run away. The truck was a stick shift, so when she would flee, she would grind the transmission to find the reverse.

I always wondered how in the world my mom and dad ever got together. I must have been adopted because there was no way on earth my parents had ever "communicated" three times. Well, at least they made up three times.

As a result of one make-up, I was born in the front seat of a 1965 Ford Falcon station wagon while enroute to the hospital. My dad was driving my mom from Midvale to Holy Cross Hospital in downtown Salt Lake City. At 7:45 p.m. that Wednesday night, my dad slowed down for a red light at the intersection of 5th South and 7th East. My mom delivered me, her six-pound fourteen-ounce baby boy, right there in the front seat. I joked later in life that I was the only child in my family to be conceived and born in that car. My dad never thought that was funny. When my dad pulled up to the Emergency Room entrance, my mom walked into the hospital holding me wrapped up in a blanket.

My brother was born in the hospital. My sister was born in the labor room without getting to the delivery room. Mom told the doctor who gave me the initial exam, "If we have any more, they'll probably be born at home." Later, when I was old enough to understand, Mom told me that she was upset when the hospital gave her a bill for the fifty-dollar delivery fee. She showed me the typed-out receipt from the Holy Cross Hospital. Yes, it said: "Delivery Room fee fifty dollars." Knowing my mom, she probably demanded a refund.

We lived in a modest, little home on Van Buren Street in the heart of Midvale. As you look east out of the kitchen window, the majestic 11,461-foot Twin Peaks of the Wasatch Mountain range are perfectly centered to fill the window frame like a postcard. Our neighborhood was filled with children. All of the homes were new. 1964, my parents bought our three-bedroom house for $13,000. It had an unfinished basement, and once I was a bit older, my room was downstairs.

I had a lot of friends in our neighborhood. I spent most of my time playing on St. Mary's Drive, which ran east up a slight hill from Van Buren Street. There were two homes on St. Mary's

Drive where I spent most of my childhood. The Haws family and the Vicchrilli family lived across the street from each other at the top of the street. Both families had seven children, so there was always someone to play with. I spent most of my time in the Haws home. I felt safe and loved there.

I vividly remember one afternoon when I was six years old when my dad returned home from work and my mom picked a routine verbal fight with him. I was so frightened that I escaped out the back door and ran up the street. I sat on the front porch of the Haws home. Sometime later, Ralph Haws, the dad, pulled into the driveway, parked the car, and came over to me. He sat beside me on the porch. He was slender, 5' 10" or so. He had jet black hair, parted on one side. He wore black, framed glasses. He was a schoolteacher and was wearing a white, short-sleeved shirt, black slacks, and dress shoes.

"What's going on?" Ralph asked.

"My mom and dad are fighting again," I said sheepishly and obviously embarrassed.

Ralph turned his head and looked down the street toward my house. "Yeah, I can hear that. Come in and have dinner with us. I'm sure it will be fine."

That was the day I secretly hoped that if something ever happened to my parents, Ralph and Connie Haws would adopt me and I could become a Haws. Through the years, Ralph became increasingly important to me. He had four sons and three daughters. One son, Marty, was one year older than me, however, we were in the same grade in school. Being born on September 7th meant that I made the deadline by just eight days and was the youngest in our school class.

It may have appeared to most people that I was always going to the Haws' to hang out with Marty. Honestly, I was just escaping from my home life to where I felt safe and loved.

All of Marty's brothers and sisters made me feel welcome and part of the family.

When I was nine years old or so, Connie, invited me to Sunday dinner for my birthday. The Haws' always had Sunday dinner followed by Family Night. This night, as I approached the dinner table, Connie directed me to the head of the table. I had never sat there before. This was Ralph's chair. I sat down and slid the heavy, wooden chair across the long, brown, 1970's shag carpet. I looked down and read the plate in front of me, "It's someone's special day. You are special." I don't remember what I ate for dinner, but I'll never forget that feeling when I read the plate. A warm sensation washed over my entire soul. I felt special. I felt loved.

Following dinner, all of us went into the front living room. Kelly, the oldest son, opened Family Night with prayer. Suzanne, the oldest daughter, read a scripture. We then sang a song. Ralph taught a lesson. Then, before the close of Family Night, Ralph picked up one of the kitchen chairs he had brought into the living room. He placed it in the middle of the room.

He looked at me and said, "It's your special day. We Haws have a tradition. On your birthday, you sit in this chair, and we do something special."

I stood up, looked around at the family, walked over to the chair, and sat down. I gripped the seat and wiggled a bit to get comfortable. I sat on my hands and looked up at Ralph. I was excited to be included in this family tradition, but I also felt uncomfortable because I didn't feel worthy to be a Haws.

"We'll go around the room, and everyone will tell you why they love you," Ralph explained.

One by one, each member of the Haws family shared why they loved me. Tears welled up in my eyes. My heart was pounding in my chest. By the time they had all shared their feelings, giant tears streamed down my cheeks. I had never felt what I felt at that moment—unconditional love—no matter what. Just thinking about that moment to this day still stirs my heart and causes a lump in my throat. That birthday was truly one of my favorites, not because of what we ate for dinner, or any presents I was given, but because I felt special and loved.

I craved the feeling I felt in the Haws home; I looked for every opportunity to be there. As we grew older, Marty excelled at sports. I wasn't athletic at all, but Ralph always found ways for me to be included right in the middle of it all. When I was eleven years old, he asked me to be his assistant coach for the team Marty was playing on in the league at the National Guard Armory in Murray. Ralph impressed me with the importance of my assignment to keep detailed statistics for him. Ralph became like my second dad and played a vital role in my childhood development. Ralph mentored me, tutored me, coached me, and always made me feel special and loved. Ralph taught me the important things in life, like how to shoot the perfect free throw.

Even though my family put the word fun in dysfunctional, that doesn't mean there weren't moments of love in my own home. It just seemed rare as a child. Holidays were bittersweet; my mom would prepare a fancy meal, and everything would seem perfect, but then something would snap, and true to form, my mom would end up speeding down Van Buren Street in a rage in the old truck. She would usually come back a few hours later after she had cooled off. However, several times she didn't come home until the next day. I often toiled with the thought, *If my mom loved me, why did she run away every time there was an issue?* At some point, I vowed I was going to break the cycle and have my own family just like the Haws family.

As I grew into my teens, I began exploring my natural gifts. I found my voice. I discovered humor was the best medicine, not just for others, but also for me. I grew in my abilities, and by the time I was thirteen, I was a professional, award-winning entertainer. I would go on to perform thousands of shows in the United States and abroad. At this point, my relationship with my mom took a dramatic turn. My mom embraced my gifts and sacrificed in every way to help me fly. She became my biggest cheerleader. I spent countless hours with my mom on the road and grew to understand her. I loved my mom, and despite a wild ride as a child, I'm extremely grateful God placed me in the Green house.

I would go on to success in broadcasting and professional speaking, but truthfully, none of that really mattered in comparison to the deep yearning I had to be married and have a happy family of my own.

In the summer of 1992, I met the woman of my dreams and was excited to live "happily ever after" together. To my utter dismay, the Disney fairytale didn't come true. One late October night in 1999, everything changed in an instant for me. I had returned home from a performance downtown. As I pulled into the driveway, I reached up and pressed the button on the visor to open the garage door. As the garage door was rolling up, I noticed my wife, Lisa's, gold Honda Accord was not in the garage. I thought for sure she would be home. It was well past our two kids' bedtimes. Megan was five years old, and Ben was almost eighteen months old.

Certainly, Lisa and the kids should be home asleep, I thought.

I parked the car, walked up the steps, and pushed the button to close the garage door.

The moment I turned the knob, I felt an overwhelming sensation of utter emptiness come over me. I couldn't breathe. I knew something was terribly wrong. The only light on in the house was the long, fluorescent light over the island counter in the kitchen. I noticed a few things were missing from the great room and the kitchen area.

I stood in the kitchen facing my greatest fear in life; Lisa had left me and had taken our children with her. My entire soul was drowning in the numbness.

I stumbled over to the green, leather sectional facing the television and fell into it. I blankly stared ahead at my reflection on the black TV screen. They say that when you are about to die, you see a high-speed replay of your life pass in front of you. As I stared into that screen, I saw a rapid replay of my marriage to Lisa.

Lisa and I had been married for seven years. We were set up on a blind date after an introduction by a mutual friend. We did "everything right" like we were expected to in our culture. We had the capacity to accomplish extraordinary things together. We should have danced together for our sixtieth anniversary as our children and grandchildren looked on. We should have lived the fairytale life, right? Lisa was everything I had ever dreamed of in a woman and a wife. Lisa was tall and stunningly beautiful, with shoulder-length, light-brown hair and striking blue eyes. She was kind, loving, patient, soft-spoken, and very smart. She worked hard as a nurse in the neurosurgery operating room at a local hospital.

Lisa is an amazing mother. I was so proud of her; no man could ask for a better woman. But I was guilty of not showing her. I had selfishly allowed water to seep into the boat, and over the years it had become too much for her to bail out by herself. It's convenient to say when life goes wrong, we are "battling our demons," but at moments like this, we are often experiencing the natural consequences of our words and actions. I was guilty of saying some rather stupid statements a few weeks earlier. I had not kept my personal saboteurs at bay, and because of this,

I had offended her deeply. That was the tipping point for Lisa. I didn't blame her one iota. I was responsible for lighting the fuse to this unimaginable nightmare for me and my family.

I sat on the couch staring at the black television screen for what seemed like hours. It was now the middle of the night and the thought of reaching out to family and friends for emotional support seemed ridiculous. Frankly, I was embarrassed and humiliated. I went to my bedroom and attempted to calm myself down by taking a long, hot shower. As I stepped out of the shower and in front of the bathroom mirror, I was still visibly shaking. The magnitude of the situation was sinking deeper. As I looked at my reflection, I was ashamed. I could not have been further from my childhood dream of having a home filled with love.

I got ready for bed, turned off the light, and stared at the ceiling until the sun filled the room.

The next morning, I called my mom and dad and told them what had happened. They had separated when I was younger for a period but ultimately got back together. My mom was supportive and assured me everything would be all right. I appreciated her optimism, but it would take a miracle to resurrect my marriage. My mom handed the phone to my dad, and I paraphrased what I had told my mom. There was a long, awkward silence.

"Dad, you there?" I asked.

"I'm sorry, son. I love you."

My body tingled from head to toe with a feeling like a million little needles were pricking my skin. Right then was the first time I could remember ever hearing my dad tell me that he loved me.

Although my life was in the proverbial crapper, a slight ray of light did shine through and touched my heart. I felt some love from my dad. It's crazy how such a devastating time could give such a gift.

My thoughts quickly returned to Lisa and our children. I was committed to trying harder and doing better, but it was too late. I was responsible for this tragedy. I had to accept the new reality that I was about to become one of those dads who takes their kids to Denny's for Thanksgiving dinner. Even the thought of that scenario made me physically ill. It's been said that discipline weighs ounces and regret weighs tons. Now, there were tons of regret weighing on my chest. So many would-ofs, could-ofs, and should-ofs. The consequences of my selfishness felt too much to bear.

I reluctantly tried to settle into the new routine of having Megan and Ben on Wednesday night and every other weekend. That schedule put me in my place. This was not what I ever imagined life would be like; not at all like the life I had dreamed of as a child growing up in Midvale, watching "normal" families with longing. But here I was, dreams shattered, enduring the consequences I feared most.

Prior to Lisa leaving, I was working nights. I would get home at 6:00 a.m., and Lisa would be getting ready to leave by 6:15 for her shift in the operating room at the hospital. This meant that I would get the kids up, get Megan ready for school, and drive her to the elementary school for half-day Kindergarten. I would play with Ben and do things around the house and then go back to school and pick up Megan at lunchtime. My days with my children were priceless to me. I shared a strong connection to my children. That's why this new arrangement stung so freaking much.

One Saturday morning in mid-November, the aroma of baking chocolate chip cookies filled the air in the house when the call came. I remember as a child standing in the kitchen wearing an old apron my mom used to wear while she made her signature bakery goods. My mom was a master baker. I would sit for hours on the bar stool at the kitchen counter and watch my mother create spectacular, multi-tiered wedding cakes and other delectable masterpieces. At those times, I did feel a special connection with my mom. I learned that my mom's secret ingredient she used in every creation was love. I associated baking with sharing love. So, that morning, as I was baking chocolate chip cookies for Megan and Ben, I tried to create some of my childhood magic for my kids.

Megan was sitting at the kitchen island counter coloring in a new coloring book I had just bought for her. I'm sure every dad believes this, but my daughter was and is to this day something very, very special. Megan's smile would melt my heart. Her eyes sparkled. Her strawberry blonde hair was cut into a perfect bob. Megan could sit for hours and color quietly.

Ben was sitting on the floor just a few feet away from me. He too was a very mild-mannered child that just melted his daddy's heart. Ben was certainly a mini-me. My baby pictures could have been of him. Before Ben was born, I had some very sensitive feelings about my son and what we should name him. I wanted to name him Benjamin Franklin Green. Benjamin Franklin was one of my heroes, and I loved the character of Benjamin Franklin "Hawkeye" Pierce on the television series M*A*S*H. Lisa wasn't fond of that full name, so we settled on Benjamin Rex Green. Rex is my middle name, so Lisa's voice of reason prevailed. I'm happy about that.

The television was on in the background with the sounds of Saturday morning cartoons. The timer on the oven dinged. I donned the big mitten hot pads and took the cookie sheet out of the oven. I grabbed a spatula and carefully slid the hot, gooey cookies onto the cooling rack.

I asked Megan to go to my bedroom and retrieve my watch from the nightstand and bring it to me. She hopped off the stool and cheerfully bounded down the hall to the bedrooms. I heard a noise, a faint yelp from the other side of the house. I wiped my hands on the dish towel and turned toward the hallway. Megan sprinted into the kitchen with a look on her face that I had never seen before: Her eyes were shining even brighter as if she had just witnessed magic.

"Daddy, Daddy," she said, sounding out of breath, "you have to come to your bedroom."

"What is it, honey?" I asked.

She came over to me, grabbed my hand, and started pulling me down the hall.

"What is it?" I asked again.

"You're not going to believe this. C'mon, Daddy, hurry."

Megan pulled my outstretched arm around the corner in the hall, stopped in the doorway of my bedroom, and pointed at the bed.

"Look Daddy, Santa Claus has been here."

Befuddled, I couldn't understand why Santa would come to our house already. Christmas was at least a month away.

Megan ran over and jumped on the bed.

"Hold on a minute, Megan. I need to go get Ben."

I ran back to the great room and scooped up Ben in my arms and returned to my bedroom. Megan was now kneeling on the bed, holding an envelope. I sat Ben on the bed beside her. I stood near the foot of the bed. The bed was loaded with Santa Claus gear. The Santa coat was bright red and appeared to be crushed velvet, with beautiful fur along the front, more fur on the collar, and circling the cuffs of the sleeves. Beside the coat, there was a pair of red trousers with suspenders attached to the waist. To top it off, there was a pair of black, spit-polished boots on the floor in front of the bed. They also had that same white fur along the top. Laying on the bed next to Megan was Santa's fur-lined hat with a white pom-pom on the end. Also on the bed was a white beard and mustache that actually looked life-like. There was a pair of gold spectacles resting between the hat and beard. Lastly, and impressively, was a large, red, velvet-like bag with a gold drawstring rope spread out, covering half the bed.

Megan chimed, "Daddy, Daddy, look what I've got. It's a letter from Santa."

"Now why would we be getting a letter from Santa?" I questioned. "We're the ones who write letters to Santa. I've never heard of him writing letters to us."

"No, Daddy, it's not to you. It says to Megan and Ben on it."

The envelope appeared to be hand-made. It was spectacular. On the vibrant, gold foil, it in fact read, "Megan and Ben." Megan turned it over to open it. It had an elegant seal of red wax with an intricate scroll pattern with the initials "S.C" stamped into it.

"What are you waiting for? Open it," I encouraged.

Megan just stared at me like a deer in the headlights, paralyzed by all the excitement. She rolled back off her knees and sat with her legs crossed. She put the envelope on her lap and carefully broke the wax seal. She stopped and looked up at me again, seeking more reassurance.

"Do it, open it," I said, nudging her with confidence.

Megan carefully lifted the flap from the envelope and slid the letter out. She set the envelope on the bed and unfolded the letter. She just stared at it and looked up again.

"What does it say, Megs?"

Although I wanted to take over and read the letter, I encouraged Megan to read it out loud to Ben and I. Slowly sounding out the words, she began reading the letter:

Dear Megan and Ben:

I am getting old, and there are more children on earth than ever before. I need help from some special helpers this year. I'm asking you both if it's okay for your daddy to be one of my special helpers. When he is not with you, he'll be with me at the North Pole getting ready for Christmas. Please write me a letter back letting me know if you'll let your daddy do it. Thank you. Merry Christmas.

Love,

Santa.

When Megan finished reading the letter, she was grinning from ear to ear.

"Santa needs your help, Daddy! You gotta help Santa! You just gotta help Santa."

"He's asking you and Ben for your permission for me to help him. The weekends you're with Mom I'd be helping Santa get ready for Christmas. Who knows, he might even need my help on Christmas Eve."

As I spoke, Megan grew even more excited. Ben crawled over on the bed and picked up the spectacles, opened them up, and tried to place them on his nose. They were too big and slipped off. We laughed out loud together.

"C'mon, Daddy, let's write a letter to Santa and tell him you're going to help him."

Megan jumped off the bed and grabbed my hand as she had just minutes before.

I laughed. "Let me grab Ben. You two can go to your room and write Santa a letter. I'll make sure he gets it tomorrow."

Megan let go of my hand and raced to her bedroom down the hall. I picked up Ben, stood him on the floor, put his hand in mine, and helped him walk to Megan's room. She was already sitting at her little play table with a blank piece of white paper and her box of crayons in front of her.

Megan carefully looked at the box of crayons and pulled out the red one. I sat Ben in the other little chair across from Megan. I knelt on the floor between them. I handed the box of crayons to Ben. He grabbed an entire fistful of crayons and dropped them on the table.

Megan paused and looked up at the ceiling, seemingly searching for inspiration. She leaned over the paper and carefully wrote in her best handwriting a letter to Santa. After a minute or two, she stopped and picked up her masterpiece.

"Well, read it to Ben and me, Megs."

She got a serious look on her face and read it out loud:

Dear Santa:

Ben and me say YES! My daddy will help you. He'll do it.

Love, Megan and Ben Green

"That's awesome, Megs. Well done. I'm proud of you."

"Ben, is it okay if I help Santa at the North Pole this year and maybe on Christmas Eve?" I asked my little buddy.

Ben just smiled and nodded. I slid Megan's letter in front of him. Ben took a crayon and made his mark. I picked up the note and reread it to myself. It was perfect. I sat the letter back down on the table in front of Megan.

"How about if you and Ben make a colorful envelope to send the letter back to Santa in? Maybe you could both draw a picture of Santa and send that too."

Megan leaned back in her chair and grabbed a couple more sheets of blank paper. She slid one piece of paper in front of Ben to keep him occupied so she could make an envelope for the reply to Santa. As Megan worked on the envelope, I watched my two children, proud of their enthusiasm for Christmas.

"Hey, Megs," I said, "can I ask you something?"

Megan looked up from her envelope-making, still holding a crayon in her hand.

"Sure, Daddy."

"What do you think Santa is up to at the North Pole today?"

Megan's eyes lit up. "Well, I think he's probably checking his list, and making sure all the elves are making toys, and taking care of the reindeer."

"Good answer, Megs. Do you think he's happy up there?"

Megan thought for a moment before responding. "I think he's happy because he loves giving presents to all the kids."

"That's true, Megs. And you know, I think Santa has a lot of love in his heart. He wants to make sure everyone is happy and loved, no matter where they are or what they're going through."

Ben looked up from his paper and grinned.

"And you know what? I think Santa has a special kind of magic. He can help us all believe in love and kindness, and remind us that we can all be helpers too."

Megan finished the envelope and handed it to me.

"Here you go, Daddy. Let's put Santa's letter and the picture in it!"

I carefully folded the letter and picture, sliding them into the envelope.

"This is going to be the best Christmas ever, Daddy," Megan said, beaming with excitement.

"I think you might be right, Megs," I replied.

I stood up and turned to walk to my bedroom. I stopped and turned around in the doorway. Megan started telling Ben all the things Daddy might help Santa with at the North Pole like decorating the Christmas tree, wrapping presents, and feeding the reindeer.

I listened, smiled, and felt peace in my heart.

～ 2 ～

BE in Tune

He who has not Christmas in his heart
will never find it under a tree.

– ROY L. SMITH

M Y HEART WAS FULL OF JOY for the experience I had just been a part of with Megan and Ben. There was a renewed connection between the kids and me. This is what being a dad is supposed to feel like. I was so proud of them.

As I returned to my bedroom, I saw two beautifully wrapped presents sitting on the nightstand. The kids and I had somehow not previously noticed them earlier when we were together in the room. An envelope like the one addressed to Megan and Ben was propped up against one of the gifts. I sat down on the bed and picked up the envelope. It was addressed to me.

Why was I receiving a letter from Santa too? I thought.

Before opening it, I sat the letter beside me on the bed, feeling drawn to the gifts. I'm horrible at not waiting to open presents on Christmas Day. When I was a child, we were allowed to open one present on Christmas Eve. I was never surprised at what I received because days before I would secretly unwrap my presents, check them out, and then carefully rewrap them so my parents didn't know they had already been opened.

These presents looked spectacular. Both were wrapped with shiny, gold paper like the envelope and had little scenes of the North Pole embossed on them. I had never seen anything as exquisite before. The pattern was so delicate, so intricate.

I picked up one of the presents. I carefully pulled one of the flaps open, then the other. I would usually just tear the wrapping paper off, but I was deliberate to preserve the paper as a keepsake. I then folded up the wrapping paper neatly and placed it back on the nightstand.

This gift was in a small box about the same size as a pencil box. The top lid was slightly larger than the bottom, so the pieces fit one into the other. I lifted the lid and found the box contained a red bag made out of the same material as the Santa suit, but it was smaller. It had a gold drawstring pulled closed. I sat the box by the wrapping paper. I pulled the little bag open, turned it upside down, and a metal object fell out on my lap. I picked up the object and held it in my open palm. It was a tuning fork. I'm not a musician, but I had seen tuning forks in the sixth grade when I was in band class. I understood what they were for, but this was a strange gift to receive from Santa. I tapped the tuning fork on the side of the nightstand and raised it to my ear. It made a beautiful tone.

Inspecting the surface of the tuning fork, I noticed at the base of the fork was an engraving with the numbers 528. I didn't have a clue what 528 meant.

I thought, *I need to research the numbers 528 to understand its significance.*

I returned the tuning fork to the small, red bag and put it in its box.

I picked up the second present. It was wrapped exactly like the first one. I unwrapped it. It was a thin, white rectangular box with the words "Top Secret" stamped in red ink on the top lid. I opened one end of the box and slid out the inner tray. The contents were protected by a thin layer of red foam rubber. I lifted the foam off. It was a red titanium smart phone; it was more advanced than anything available on the consumer market. I pressed the power button on the side. As it powered up, a scene from the North Pole appeared, complete with falling snow and the sound of jingle bells. Once it was completely powered up, it displayed one large app in the center of the screen. It was labeled simply "SC."

"Holy whip. This is a special phone with a direct connection to Santa Claus," I exhaled out loud.

Now I just had to read the letter from Santa and connect the dots. I picked up the envelope and opened it with care. I wanted to save this too. I pulled the letter out from the envelope, unfolded it, and noticed it was a full page written in smaller handwriting than the kids' letter. I began reading.

Dear Coz,

I've been watching you. I'm aware of your pain and anguish. I'd like to say I feel bad for you, however, your current troubles are your own doing.

I tried to swallow the lump in my throat that was growing with each word I read, then continued.

You, my friend, are out of tune. You are in
dissonance from the power within your soul.
I've given you a tuning fork and challenge
you to discover what its frequency means.

I didn't have a clue what Santa was saying. What did he mean
I was out of tune? How was I in dissonance?

You're a good man, a special soul. You have
amazing, unique gifts and talents. A combina-
tion of which not many possess; but you have
lost sight of what is most important in your
life and have failed to be a good steward of
what you have been blessed with. You have
achieved many successes in your professional
life. But as the English Prime Minister Benjamin Disraeli once wrote, "No success in public
life can compensate for failure in the home."

I looked away. *Ouch*, I thought.

"That is bold. Who does Santa think he is talking to me like
this?" I wanted to stop reading, but I couldn't. He was right,
and the truth hurt.

Your greatest desire in life has been to have
a happy family filled with laughter and love.
You've lost that for now. Don't make excuses;
excuses don't change performance.

The lump in my throat was now a pit in my stomach. Santa
does watch our actions, and we can't hide. Then, the tone of the
letter changed and became somewhat philosophical.

Nikola Tesla wrote, "*If you want to find the secrets of the Universe, think in terms of energy, frequency, and vibration.*" You are out of tune with the frequency of your best self. I'm calling you to be one of my few, very special ambassadors of love and light. There are many who wear my suit and do good things for Christmas. But I have chosen you as one capable of doing this at the highest level. So, level up; no more excuses.

I had never thought of Santa as a great teacher, but he's seen it all, so it's logical he would be an expert on all of this. I read on:

I'm concerned about what is happening in the world today. Too many people have lost the true spirit of Christmas. All I hear is children wanting iPhones, iPads, ithis, and ithat. Everything is I, I, I. That's not what Christmas is all about. The Christmas Spirit is not about what you can get, but what you can give.

A bell is no bell until you ring it,

a song is no song until you sing it,

and love in your heart wasn't put there to stay.

Love isn't love, until you give it away.

- Oscar Hammerstein II

We have become selfish people, thinking only of ourselves. That won't end well.

My vision became blurry as tears flooded my eyes. Santa does more than observe our behaviors. I realized at that moment something even more important: He knows our hearts. I wiped a tear off my cheek and continued.

It has become a tradition over time for my helpers to sit for pictures and ask children what they want for Christmas. There is nothing wrong with that; that is good. It helps children be on the "nice list" to get what they want. However, you will proclaim a different message. A more important one. Instead of asking children what they want for Christmas, you will ask them what they are going to give for Christmas. This may seem ludicrous to the world. Some may resist the change; if so, they are out of tune themselves.

The truth is that the real gifts of Christmas cannot be bought in a store and wrapped with a bow. The real gifts of Christmas are shared from the heart and given with love. Be courageous and bold. Share this magical message with the world: *Be less selfish, be more elfish*. All of us at the North Pole are the happiest people on the planet because we live this way every day. We are elfish. It's the standard. Can you imagine the world we would live in if we lived the spirit of Christmas all year round? The world would be a different place, indeed. Think about how the

Spirit of Christmas feels. Folks strive to be more kind, more loving, more charitable. Consider that magical spirit living on if we would live that way each day. I'm calling you to start a movement, to find those who will accept the challenge to be different, to live life striving to be more elfish!

The weight of what Santa was asking me to do began to sink in and weighed heavy on my shoulders. Who was I to do what he was asking? Santa was asking me to break tradition. Plus, he knew what I had been going through. He knew my struggles. I didn't think I was in a state of mind to accept his call. I doubted Santa had chosen the right guy for the job.

Simply putting on a suit doesn't make me Santa, I thought. And just as if he read my thoughts, he went on:

Being Santa Claus is much more than wearing a red suit. Anyone can wear a suit and act like me. But BEing Santa comes from the heart. You must connect with people on the frequency of the tuning fork I gave you. No, it won't be easy. The best things in life aren't easy, but I promise you it will be worth it.

I lay back on the bed and stared at the ceiling, clutching the letter to my chest. I closed my eyes and took some deep breaths. Slowly, a calm, peaceful feeling filled my entire soul. In my mind, I could see people around the world from a different perspective. I could see families of different cultures coming together as a worldwide family. I could see each person I encountered with new eyes. I realized what I was seeing was as if through Santa's eyes. I only saw the goodness in people. I wasn't judging them. I wasn't focused on their differences. I saw their similarities as human beings; no one person was better than another. I saw their unique strengths and what they were capable of. I just lay there and marinated in this warm feeling and the new perspective I could see. I got it. That's what Santa meant about being elfish. It's not something you DO, it's who you ARE.

I opened my eyes and sprung upright.

The letter concluded:

I believe in you. You are enough. Onward and upward, my friend.

With love,

Santa.

P.S. In time, as you have eyes to see, you will have the courage and strength to fulfill the mission for which you were created.

I carefully folded up Santa's letter and slid it back into the envelope. The magnitude of his calling was overwhelming. I was being asked to not just spread a message, but to lead a movement and change the way some of Santa's helpers spread the Spirit of Christmas. Me. He was asking me. That would require me to make significant changes in my own life first. I couldn't give anything away that I didn't possess first.

I pulled the tuning fork back out of the little, red bag. I looked at the engraving again and traced it with my right index finger. 5-2-8. I took a deep breath and exhaled with a different feeling in my heart than I'd had in the kitchen baking cookies just an hour prior. I had a glimmer of hope that life could be better. My heart burned with a desire to be less selfish and be more elfish.

I wanted to use the new phone and call Santa, but I didn't feel I was ready. I stood and picked up the Santa suit from off the bed. I slid my fingers over it to feel the shimmery, crushed velvet, red coat. I carried the suit into the walk-in closet, grabbed a wooden suit hanger, and placed it on the rail. I retrieved the rest of Santa's gear and put it on the top shelf of the closet.

I turned and walked out of the closet. Megan was standing in the doorway of the bedroom. She had been watching me read Santa's letter and saw me put his gear away in the closet.

"Daddy, I have a question," she said.

"Okay, give it to me, Megs."

"How many continents are there?" she asked.

I chuckled. "That's a big question. Where did you learn about continents?"

"At school, Daddy," she said, rolling her eyes like I should just know that.

"There are seven continents, Megs." I listed the seven continents of the world for Megan.

"Oh, so you're the Santa for North America. I get it now," she said as though she had just unlocked a secret Santa code of how the big guy visits the entire planet on Christmas Eve.

I knelt down and gave Megan a big squeeze. There is absolutely nothing better than a hug from one of your children. As I held Megan in my arms, I reflected on the letter and gifts from Santa. I had mixed emotions; I was excited about the pending adventures, but I was anxious about finding this frequency Santa said I needed to BEcome one of his chosen helpers.

~ 3 ~

BEcoming Santa

It doesn't matter who you used to be;
what matters is who you decide to be today.

– BRITTANY JOSEPHINA

ON MONDAY MORNING, I stood alone in front of the bathroom mirror. I had dropped Megan and Ben off the night before to be with Lisa until Wednesday night. This was the moment of truth. I looked myself in the eyes in the mirror.

I asked myself, "Could I actually BE Santa? Could I get in tune with this 'frequency' he was talking about? Could I develop the courage to lead this new movement? Could I become less selfish and be more elfish myself?"

The Santa suit was now hanging on the towel rack, all of the gear was laid out on the vanity, and the boots were on the floor beside me.

"Well, here goes nothing," I sighed.

I slid each leg into the trousers and pulled the suspenders up and over my shoulders. The trousers fit perfectly, as though they had been custom-tailored for me. Of course, they had been. Those elves at the North Pole are good. I took the coat from the hanger and put it on; again, it was a perfect fit. I put on the white beard, which went down past my chin to the bottom of my neck. I was starting to look like Santa. I attached the mustache to my upper lip with some liquid adhesive and arranged it so it was straight. Then I pulled the wig over my forehead and slid it down the back of my head. There were two small sideburns which I tugged on to align it with everything else. I finally placed the cap on my head and arranged it just so.

I stood there and studied my new look. Yes, I kind of looked like Santa, but I didn't feel like Santa. I gripped the top of each boot and stepped in, first my left foot and then my right. I stood straight and tall. Something was missing. I looked down at the vanity. Santa's gold spectacles were sitting there folded up.

Ah, I knew I was missing something, I thought.

I unfolded the spectacles, placed them on my nose, and tucked the side pieces behind my ears.

"Now we're cooking."

As I looked through those spectacles, I saw myself differently. But more importantly, I felt different. Seeing through Santa's perspective changed my feelings. It was pure magic what happened when I wore Santa's spectacles.

Donning all of Santa's gear, I headed straight to the basement to do some research. I turned on the light in my home office and recording studio. I fired up the computer. As the computer booted up, I could see my reflection in the blank monitor.

"I am Santa Claus," I said out loud. "I am Santa Claus. I am Santa Claus."

I looked like Santa Claus, and I felt like Santa Claus. I thought I knew the history of the North Pole and Santa Claus, but to BE Santa, I better have my facts straight.

I opened a browser window and searched, "The history of the North Pole and Santa Claus."

The search returned thousands of links to articles and stories. I travelled down the rabbit holes and read for hours.

I opened up a new document in Word and wrote my own version as a composite of the history of the North Pole and Santa Claus.

I simply dictated what flowed through me.

For generations, the North Pole has been associated with Santa Claus, a mythical figure celebrated in many Western holiday traditions. The story of how he came to be linked to this polar region has changed over the centuries.

The description of the jolly figure known as Santa Claus originates from the tale of Saint Nicholas, a Christian cleric who lived during the fourth century in present-day Turkey. He was highly respected for his kindheartedness and benevolence toward children. People around Europe soon began to celebrate December 6th as a celebration in his honor, where they gave gifts to one another.

The transformation of Saint Nicholas into the modern Santa Claus began in the seventeenth century in Europe. Dutch settlers brought this tradition to the Americas and called him "Sinterklaas." On December 5th, he would visit homes and leave gifts for children. This is how Santa Claus was born.

In the early 1800s, all the pieces of what came to be known as the Santa Claus legend began to amalgamate in America. Washington Irving's 1809 piece, "Knickerbocker's History of New York," was a big part of this, introducing the character of Saint Nicholas as someone who smoked a pipe and flew around in a wagon. To solidify this image even further, Clement Clarke Moore's 1823 poem, "A Visit from St. Nicholas," also called "The Night Before Christmas," made him out to be jolly and round-bellied, traveling in an airborne sleigh with reindeer.

It was in the late nineteenth century that Santa Claus came to be associated with the North Pole, largely due to the work of Thomas Nast's illustrations for Harper's Weekly and Coca-Cola's famous Christmas advertisements. Nast showed Santa in his workshop filled with elves at the North Pole, and this image caught on. Later, Coca-Cola's ads featured a rotund St. Nick wearing red in the North Pole, helping to firmly establish this spot as his home in the public imagination.

Today's popular culture depicts the North Pole as Santa Claus' traditional home, where he, along with his loyal band of elves, toil year-round in preparation for Christmas. Kiddos worldwide wait anxiously for his arrival on Christmas Eve to share merriment and deliver presents.

Where Santa Claus came from is a story that has many different parts. Nevertheless, the North Pole still embodies his fantastic abode where joy and kindness are seen during the Christmas season.

Santa's a legend. I've got big shoes to fill, I thought.

I reread my overview five or six times to commit it to memory. Even if I was grilled by the smartest ten-year-old interrogator, I was now prepared.

I still had a lingering question in the back of my mind. Santa said to BE him, I had to "be in tune" and be on the right frequency. The tuning fork was engraved with the numbers 5-2-8. Did he make it that easy for me, or was it just a clue to lead me down more rabbit holes on the internet?

I opened a new search in the browser. I typed "528 frequency" and hit enter. Thank goodness Al Gore invented the internet and made it so easy.

I began reading the search results. It all sounded like Yiddish to me.

Oh great, this is all about science and math, not exactly my strongest subjects, I thought.

Then, I read a paragraph that summed it all up simply and beautifully:

> The number 528 is measured in hertz (Hz) and stands for the amount of times something can oscillate or go through a cycle within one second. This special frequency is known as "The Frequency of Love."

I took a deep breath. Santa told me in his letter that I wasn't in tune with this frequency. Had I hardened my heart to love? Was that why Lisa left? Had my lack of love led to my selfishness? I reflected on these questions and had to come to terms with the answers. Yes, my lack of love for myself and others had affected my words and actions. I was not sending the frequency of love. My selfishness also repelled me from receiving love. That is a bitter pill to swallow.

I read more and discovered that everything on earth has a frequency, a vibration. 528 is a frequency and vibration also in the light spectrum. What color is 528 in the light spectrum? Yep, green. Do your own homework. You'll be blown away.

Here's a simple way of understanding frequency and vibration. If I hold a tuning fork that is tuned to the note of "C" and hit it with an object, it will vibrate in that frequency. If I take that vibrating tuning fork and hold it over the strings of a grand piano, the strings of C will now also vibrate, not A, B, D, E, F, or G. Just the note of C. Have you ever met a person or walked into a room, and it just didn't feel right? That's frequency.

I learned about vibration years ago when I worked with Brian Tracy. I memorized all of the immutable, universal laws. The Law of Attraction says that we are all living magnets, that we attract people, opportunities, and circumstances in harmony with who we are. But now it made even more sense to me; I was seeing it through a new lens. If I was going to BE Santa, BE a good dad, and BE a better person, it was one hundred percent up to me to change my frequency. I accepted the challenge right there, right then.

Now, I need to get in front of people this Christmas and share the message. Maybe I should use the phone Santa gave me and ask him what to do next, I thought.

I've been a professional entertainer since the early 1980s and performed in front of audiences around the world. So, I know how to market entertainment and make the phone ring. I opened a new document on my computer and titled the document, "The Movement." I closed my eyes, said a quick silent prayer, and then dictated what came through me. A two-page document flowed from my fingertips. I reread it; it was word perfect.

I now looked like Santa Claus. I felt like Santa Claus. I had a plan to get Santa Claus in front of as many people as I could this holiday season. As the great prophet Nike once said, "Just do it." I took massive action and just did it.

~ 4 ~

My Little Brother

*Santa Claus is anyone who loves another and seeks
to make them happy; who gives himself by thought
or word or deed in every gift that he bestows.*

– EDWIN OSGOOD GROVER

THANKSGIVING DAY came and went. Megan and Ben were
with Lisa for the holiday. It was heartbreaking and lonely.
This was the worst possible time to be without my family. To
say that I was suffering from the consequences of my words is
an understatement.

My extended family and my closest friends tried to invite me
to a few activities, but nothing could fill the hole in my heart.

I muddled through the challenging Thanksgiving holiday
weekend. On Monday morning, my thoughts turned to "The
Movement" plan. I had executed my plan, and my calendar was
getting packed with Santa Claus appearances.

My first appearance as Santa was scheduled for next Friday
night at the Salt Palace Convention Center for the Children's
Miracle Network. There's nothing like baptism by fire, right?

Throughout the week, I struggled with putting my Santa routine together. I wanted to rehearse something. I kept drawing a blank. I'd performed thousands of shows throughout the planet, but this was different. I needed to be more than a Santa sitting in the mall for pictures. These men do noble and sacred work. But I needed to BE one of his chosen few that reached thousands of people each season. The magnitude of what Santa had called me to do was sinking deep.

Friday night finally came. I arrived at the convention center early and just sat in my car. My heart was doing the four-minute mile. I closed my eyes and uttered a simple prayer to God expressing my gratitude for the call from Santa and now the opportunity to start the movement. I asked God to bless me with the words to say, at the right moment, that would do the most good.

"God, this movement is not about me, it's about thee." The moment I said that out loud, my heart rate slowed to normal, and my anxiety vanished.

I heard a still, small voice that seemed to come from the middle of my heart. I felt it as much as I heard it.

"Be natural. Let it flow. You can't force it," the voice whispered.

"Amen," I concluded.

I opened the car door, grabbed my big toy bag, and rushed confidently toward the backstage door where I had been instructed to meet my liaison with the organization.

As I stopped to open the door, it swung wide open, and a woman filled the doorway.

"Hi, Santa, I'm Karen Miller. I'll be your helper tonight," she said with a huge smile as she shook my hand.

"I'm honored to be here. Thank you for the invitation," I said and detected a slight difference in my voice as I spoke. Maybe I just needed a drink of water.

"In about ten minutes, I'll lead you to the backstage area where the program is going on in the main convention hall," Karen instructed. "You have about twenty-five minutes for your show, and then we'll just play it by ear after that. Sound good?"

"Let's go make some magic," I said to Karen.

I stood backstage for what seemed more like an hour than ten minutes. Finally, it was showtime. The emcee explained to the audience that a special guest had flown in from the North Pole and was there to be a part of their special event. Karen reached out and drew the curtain back for me to step out onto the stage.

"Ladies and gentleman and all you special kids out there, help me welcome Santa Claus," the emcee announced.

Music started playing. The crowd erupted with energy. They were loud and excited. As I stepped forward on the stage, two spotlights hit me directly in the face. All I could see were the two lights. I had no idea what the size of the audience was. I stepped forward to the edge of the stage to where I could make out shapes and faces. The main hall was filled to capacity with several thousand people. I could faintly make out two television cameras in the back of the hall. A cameraman was kneeling in the aisle in front of the stage. The red light was illuminated on top of his camera. I looked directly into the camera and began speaking.

What happened next was simply divine. I honestly don't have a clue what I said. I wasn't speaking, Santa was.

My eyes became adjusted to the light. I could see thousands of eyes looking at me. But I could feel thousands of souls on the same frequency. Unless you've had the experience of that many eyes looking at you with such magical belief, you can never comprehend the electricity that surges through your soul.

I let go and let it flow.

We sang Christmas songs together. I had children from the audience come on stage to help in a couple of the numbers. I told some fun stories about life at the North Pole. As I opened my heart to the audience, I felt the most beautiful feeling. The room felt warmer. Not like an uncomfortable heat, but a warmth that touches your soul. I could actually feel these people and had a sense of their stories and why the children were here. I took the microphone and walked down the stairs into the center aisle. Now I could really see their faces. I saw moms and dads, grandmas and grandpas of every variety. I then looked at the children throughout the audience. I instantly felt which ones were the beneficiaries of the mission of the organization. It was as if I knew them each personally and could empathize with the conditions they were battling.

Then I received the prompting loud and clear, "It's time to wrap it up with the challenge."

I said, "We've been busier than ever before up at the North Pole this year. There are more children on the earth than ever. Many of you didn't waste any time sending me your Christmas wish list. Some of you had your Christmas lists to me by last Valentine's Day. You're asking for all of the popular things; many of you are asking for iPads, iPhones, ithis and ithat. When did Christmas become all about 'I'? What has happened to us and we?"

Dead silence filled the convention hall. I had their undivided attention.

"I'm the happiest man on the planet, and my elves are that happiest little people you'll ever meet. Why? Because we focus on giving, not getting. If you want to be happy this Christmas, I challenge you to ..." I paused briefly, hoping this next part would land perfectly. "**BE LESS SELFISH. BE MORE ELFISH!**" I said with a cheer.

There was a brief hush while they processed what I'd said, so I said it again. "If you want to be happy, **BE LESS SELFISH, AND BE MORE ELFISH.**"

The crowd erupted with a cheer. They understood what I was saying.

"So, if we want to be happy, BE LESS SELFISH …" I paused.

The entire audience chanted in unison, "BE MORE ELFISH!"

"Be more what?"

"Be more elfish!" they said with a roar.

I took the risk to say the mantra and it had landed perfectly. Up until that time, I'd never experienced a connection with an audience like that. I was excited, yet humbled. I felt a peace in my soul I had been missing for too long. The audience was on a frequency that I was now in resonance with. I walked back up the aisle toward the stage and climbed the stairs.

The emcee met me center stage, took the mic from me, and said, "Give it up for the one, the only Santa Claus."

I turned and blew the crowd a kiss and clapped for them. I gave a big wave and then ducked through the curtain Karen was holding open for me.

"Wow, that was amazing, Santa. I've never seen anything like that before."

"Me neither," I said. I was as surprised as Karen.

Karen led me backstage to get a drink of water and sit down for a few minutes so they could conclude the event and allow people to leave.

I took big gulps of water. I hadn't noticed how thirsty I was. I was in a zone where I didn't sense any of that. The ice-cold water ripped down my throat. I sat backstage for a few more minutes when I turned to my right and noticed there was a gap between the pipe and drape. A little girl, perhaps nine or ten years old, was waiting patiently outside of the curtain, holding hands with a little boy.

I waved to the girl and motioned for her to come backstage so we could talk. She was a beautiful little girl all dressed up for the occasion. The little boy was four years old or so. He was thin, bald, and didn't have much color on his face. I knew his condition was terminal. I felt a special connection with the little boy as our gazes met. He looked into my eyes with such love and belief. I smiled at him. I then looked up at the little girl. Her eyes sparkled with love for the little boy.

The little girl let go of the little boy's hand and stepped closer to me. We were nearly nose to nose. She looked deep into my eyes.

"Santa, all I want for Christmas is for you to make my little brother all better. I don't want him to die," she whispered in the voice of an angel.

She didn't break eye contact, waiting for my response. What in the world was I supposed to say in this moment? I couldn't make a promise he would be healed and be better. I paused and pleaded silently for the words to say. I reached out my arms and pulled them both in for a group hug. They both wrapped their arms around me and squeezed me tight. I sniffled to clear my sinuses. We let go of each other, and both children waited for me to speak.

"God bless you both. I love you. Take good care of each other," I said.

The little girl smiled at me. "Thank you, Santa. We will."

She reached down and took her little brother by the hand and headed for the curtain to exit. As they went to slide between the curtains, the little boy looked back at me, smiled, and gave me a wave with his free hand.

The convention hall was buzzing with all kinds of ambient noise from the crowd leaving the event. But during that moment with the children, time stood still; there wasn't any noise, only pure peace and love.

I hoped I'd said the right thing to the children. There wasn't going to be a do over. I picked up my big toy bag and slipped out the back door of the building.

I got in my car, put on my seat belt, and started the ignition. There was a glow coming from the passenger seat. It was the illuminated screen of the phone Santa had given me. I unlocked the screen and read the text.

Well done. That was perfect. –Santa

~ 5 ~

Captain Murphy

Christmas is not a time or season, but a state of mind.

– CALVIN COOLIDGE

I WAS WOKEN by the ringtone of "Jingle Bells" coming from Santa's phone on the nightstand.

"Good morning," I said, knowing that the big guy himself was on the other end of the line.

"Good morning to you, Coz," Santa said with a jolly chuckle. "Well, how's it going?" he asked.

"This is harder than I thought it would be," I replied.

"How so?" he asked.

"I'm usually never at a loss for what to say. Last night with those two children really kicked my keister, Santa."

"Sometimes you don't need to say anything. Just being there can be enough," Santa explained. "You're learning to listen with your heart, not your ears. You're re-learning to meet people where they are and just BE present in the moment."

"Thank you, Santa," I said.

"I have an assignment for you today. We just received an email up here at the North Pole from a Captain in the U.S. Air Force serving in South Korea. He just found out that he won't be home for Christmas with his family. He is concerned for his six-year-old son, Sean. This will be the first year Sean hasn't had his daddy home for Christmas with him. I'll forward the email to your phone so you can have all the details. I need you to go visit Sean today at his elementary school in a town called Clinton," Santa instructed.

"You bet your bippy, Santa. I've got this."

"Have a beautiful day, Coz."

"You too."

I pulled up the email Santa had forwarded to me:

Dear Santa,

It's been a while since I've written to you, but it's a special time of year and I'm hoping you can help me out. I'm a Captain in the US Air Force, and I'm stationed in South Korea. I was due to come home for Christmas this year to spend time with my family, but I'm not able to make it back home in time. It's been a difficult year for all of us, and my family has been especially affected by me being so far from home.

My son, Sean, is six years old, and he's in the first grade. I know that he's been looking forward to spending the holidays with me. I'm not sure if you can help, but I'm writing to ask if you could make a special visit to Sean's school and Mrs. Anderson's class. Please give Sean a big hug from his daddy and tell him I love him and that I'm not going to be home for Christmas this year.

I know this is a lot to ask of you, and it's certainly not a typical request. I know that it doesn't make up for me not being able to come home for Christmas, but if it's possible, I'd be deeply grateful.

If you can't make it to the school, I understand. It would mean a lot to me if he could hear it come from you. I'll be home as soon as I can.

Thank you for taking the time to read my letter. I hope you can help me out, but either way, I wish you a Merry Christmas and a Happy New Year.

Sincerely,

Captain Patrick Murphy

U.S.A.F.

I closed the email, looked up the phone number to the school, and made arrangements to visit Mrs. Anderson's class that afternoon.

When I arrived at the school, it was like something out of a movie; I walked resplendently dressed in Santa's iconic red suit covered in white fur trimming with the toy bag full of treats slung over my shoulder.

I checked in at the main office and was greeted with a warm welcome. Captain Murphy had also given the school a heads-up of my visit.

I walked down the empty hall looking for room eleven. I stood at the door and leaned in to listen. I could faintly hear Mrs. Anderson teaching a lesson. I waited for a good time to make my entrance.

I slowly opened the door just a crack and peeked in. I looked around the room and saw Mrs. Anderson standing in front of the class. All of the kids had their backs to me. I opened the door a little wider to expose my face. Mrs. Anderson smiled at me and gave me an inconspicuous nod. I swung the door wide open and let out a mighty, "Ho, ho, ho!"

Thirty-five little heads spun around in a split second.

"Santa, Santa, Santa!" they all cheered.

As I walked my way up the aisle to the front of the room, all of the kids raised their hands, begging for a high-five. I slapped high-fives as I strolled up the aisle to the front. Mrs. Anderson greeted me with an outstretched arm.

"Where's my high-five, Santa?" she asked.

"Right here!" I exclaimed.

Mrs. Anderson and I exchanged a perfect high-five complete with a loud clap of our hands together. The children laughed with delight.

"Boys and girls, we are so excited to have Santa here all the way from the North Pole. He's really busy this time of the year. I need you to show Santa your best manners while he's here, please. Can you do that?"

She turned with an open hand, pointing for me to come over to where she was and take over. I pulled a chair over to the middle of the front of the room.

"Wheeeeeew! What a ride! I need to sit down for a few minutes," I explained.

I slowly slumped into the chair like an old man trying to keep my balance.

"I was just over in South Korea picking up Barbie parts so the elves can make all of those Barbies you have on your Christmas lists. Yep, Barbies are still popular this year at the North Pole. Why, I can still remember delivering Mrs. Anderson's Barbie when she was just a wee girl."

I turned to Mrs. Anderson, who was sitting at her desk listening to me just as intently as all of the children. She smiled and nodded.

"You were like five when I delivered your first Barbie, if I remember right."

"Yes, it was," Mrs. Anderson agreed.

"Well, it's not every day you get a visit from the real Santa. I have a lot of helpers you'll see around the holidays, but let me share a few things you might not know that only the real Santa will tell you."

Some of the children rose on their knees and leaned in to listen.

"This year, I'll be starting my Christmas deliveries in Ireland, so that means I'll be here in Clinton two hours earlier than usual. That means that all good boys and girls must be in bed asleep by. . ." I paused.

"Ten o'clock, midnight, 2:00 a.m.," all the children started yelling out what time I would be to their house.

I placed my right index finger to my lips, requesting silence. They obliged.

"Eight o'clock," I said.

"What? Wait. No. That's too early, Santa," the room erupted with an objection to my timing.

"That's the only way I can give your parents what they want for Christmas, and that's a silent night, ho, ho, ho!"

Mrs. Anderson stood up and applauded me. "Yes, yes," she said.

"Now, I appreciate all of the cookies and treats you leave out for me and the reindeer on Christmas Eve. I especially love those oatmeal raisin cookies one of you left out last year. Well done. But I must tell you when I got back to the North Pole on Christmas morning, my stomach was a little sour. So, I went to Rudolph's vet, and we ran a few tests. We discovered that I'm lactose intolerant; you'll have to ask your parents what that means. Basically, somebody left out some spoiled milk, and it got me. This year I can only have three drinks in my diet. First, apple juice. Second, orange juice. Or, third, Diet Dr. Pepper 'cause where I fly at 70,000 feet, that gives me quite a buzz."

Mrs. Anderson laughed at that one and just shook her head at me with a big smile on her face.

"You know, we have been so busy up at the North Pole working our little elf fingers to the bone. We haven't had time to sing any Christmas songs together yet. Nothing puts me in the Christmas spirit faster than hearing beautiful children sing Christmas songs. Who has a favorite Christmas song?"

The entire room erupted in raised hands.

"I do. I do. I do, Santa," they all yelled.

I pressed my finger to my lips again. They all went completely silent.

"I pick my helpers from those who are showing me their best manners. They are sitting on their sit-down bones ..."

The room shifted as all of the children sat back down on their pockets.

"They have their arms folded ..."

All of the children couldn't fold their arms fast enough.

"And their mouth is filled with marshmallows."

I closed my mouth and filled my cheeks with bulging air.

All of the children took a deep breath and puffed out their cheeks.

"Yes, Mrs. Anderson, you can use this after I leave too."

I had no doubt she could now use this Santa technique to quiet the room.

I looked around the room and selected a little girl to come up to the front of the room with me.

"Let's see, you are ..."

"Laura!" she said.

"I know your name is Laura. Of course, I know everyone's name. Laura, I barely recognized you. You were only ..." I held my hand out at about half her height. "My, how you've grown this past year," I said.

Laura shrugged and looked confident with her growth.

"Laura, what's your favorite Christmas song?"

"Jingle Bells!" she blurted out.

I took the wristband of bells that I had on my left wrist and slipped it onto her left wrist and shook the bells.

"Now Laura, when we say the words 'jingle bells,' I want you to ring these bells as loudly as you can, okay? You got it?"

Laura nodded.

We sang Jingle Bells together. The children were so engaged and enjoyed it.

"Okay, who else has a favorite Christmas song?"

"I do. I do. I do, Santa," they all screamed in a somewhat controlled manner.

I folded my arms and puffed out my cheeks. The room went completely silent as the children followed my lead.

"How about you, young man?" I said, holding out an open palm, pointing toward a boy in the fourth row to my right.

"Me?" the boy said, pointing to himself.

"Yes, you. Come up here and join old Santa."

He stood by my side.

"Sean, what is your favorite Christmas song?"

Sean looked at me in amazement that I really did know his name without me asking.

"Rudolph the Red Nosed Reindeer," he responded.

"Rudolph the Red Nosed Reindeer? Why does Rudolph get all the attention? There's nine other members on the reindeer team, but yet Rudy gets all of the credit."

The children started counting on their fingers and naming all of the reindeer.

"There are only eight other reindeer on your team Santa," one boy shouted from the back row.

"I'm pleased to announce that today I have all ten reindeer with me outside," I said.

The room filled with mumbles of, "Ten?"

"Let's sing the song about old Rudy. That's what we call him at the North Pole. Hey Rudy, do you want to play any reindeer games? Hey, Rudy, go long! We'll sing Rudy's song and listen carefully and see if you can hear all of the reindeer's names."

We all started singing together, "You know Dasher and Dancer and Prancer and Vixen, Comet and Cupid and Donder"—yes, it's Donder, trust me, I know—"and Blitzen, but do you recall the most famous reindeer of all ..."

As we said the reindeer names, the children were counting on their little fingers. There is nothing sweeter than hearing children singing with such gusto!

"All of the other reindeer used to laugh and call him names." They stopped counting on their fingers and looked a little perplexed. They kept singing, "he'll go down in history." A few chimed in at the end, "like Columbus!" Giggles filled the room.

"Well, did you hear all ten of their names?" I asked.

"No, Santa, there are only nine when you include Rudolph," one child said.

"Let's see ..."

I put my hand out in front of me and started counting on my fingers as I said their names.

"Dasher, Dancer, Prancer, Vixen, Comet, Cupid, Donder and Blitzen ... and Rudy. Did anyone hear the name of the 'other' reindeer?"

All of the children looked at each other as though I was crazy.

"Olive!" I exclaimed.

Then I sang the line from the song while snapping my fingers. "Olive the OTHER reindeer used to laugh and call him names ..."

The room erupted in a collective, "Boo, Santa," as they pointed down with their thumbs.

I leaned back and let out a full belly laugh, "Ho, ho, ho." They knew Santa had tricked them. They mumbled, agreeing it was kind of funny, kind of.

The kids became quiet, and I stood beside Sean and put my arm around him and rested it on his shoulder.

"We've had some fun today, but I'm here to deliver a very special message to Sean," I said.

I knelt so my eyes were at the same height as Sean's. I turned to him so we were face to face.

"Sean, I mentioned earlier that I was over in South Korea picking up Barbie parts. Well, I also stopped by the PX—oh, a military department-type store—to pick up some treats for me and the reindeer when I ran into a guy named Captain Patrick Murphy."

Sean's eyes nearly popped out of his head when he heard me say the name. "That's my daddy," he said in utter disbelief. "How is my daddy doing?" he asked with a growing slobber to his speech.

As he looked into my eyes, I could see the very special relationship that little boy had with is daddy.

"He's doing so well, Sean," I said.

I looked over at Mrs. Anderson, and she was wiping a tear from her eye quickly so the children wouldn't see.

I turned back and squared up to Sean.

"Your daddy and I were talking, and he told me he had just received some news from his boss. He asked me if I would fly here immediately and give you the news personally. Your daddy is going to call you right when you get home from school today and tell you the news, but he wanted me to come to school, tell you in person, and give you something."

Sean didn't move a muscle.

"Your daddy has to do something really important in South Korea on Christmas Day, so he won't be home to share it with you, but he will be home as soon as he can. He wanted me to tell you face-to-face that he loves you and he is very proud of you." My voice quivered near the end of my message.

Sean wrapped his arms around me and held me tight. I could hear a faint whimper from our embrace. I held him tight too, and just let it be for a few seconds.

Sean stepped back from me, wiped the tears from his eyes, and said, "It's okay, we'll have Christmas again when my daddy gets home."

"Yes Sean, Christmas is a celebration you can have with your daddy when he gets home. Christmas doesn't have to be on a specific date on the calendar. It's a special day we share with those we love."

I stood up and smiled down at Sean.

"I'm very proud of Sean's daddy for the important things he is doing for our country—for all of us. I am grateful for Sean's daddy for the sacrifices he is making for our freedom. We can all be proud."

Mrs. Anderson was caught up in the moment and simply nodded.

"All of us at the North Pole are proud of you, and we love you Sean," I said.

Sean looked up at me and shared a radiant smile.

"Let's put our hands together for Sean's daddy and Sean for being so brave," I invited.

All of the children and Mrs. Anderson clapped and cheered for Sean as he walked back to his chair.

I picked up my bag and sat it on the table at the front of the room. I reached in and pulled out a wrapped box of treats.

"I brought all of you a treat that I'll leave with Mrs. Anderson. Sean can pass them out to you when you leave for the day," I said.

I looked at Sean to make sure he was fine. He was smiling and looked happy.

"Send me off with a mighty grand finale," I said.

I raised my arms like a maestro conducting them as a choir.

"We wish you a Merry Christmas, we wish you a Merry Christmas ... and a happy neeeeeeew yeeeeaaaaar," we sang, holding the last two words for effect.

I grabbed my empty bag, swung it over my shoulder, and waved to everyone as I back peddled out of the classroom. I stopped at the door and exclaimed, "Merry Christmas, and may this next year be your very best year yet!"

"Bye, Santa. See you soon, Santa. I love you, Santa," said the children as I closed the door.

Later that night as I was plugging in my Santa phone, I received an email forwarded to me from the North Pole.

Dear Santa,

I can't thank you enough for making a stop to see my boy, Sean, and deliver my special message. I talked to him on the phone when he got home from school. He was so excited that Santa Claus came to his class and delivered such important news in person. You made my day. You made my Christmas special. Thank you again, and God bless.

Love,

Captain Patrick Murphy
U.S.A.F.

～ 6 ～

The Puzzle

The best of all gifts around any Christmas tree: the presence of a happy family all wrapped up in each other.

– BILL VAUGHAN

From: Natalie Kershaw

Sent: Thursday, December 10 11:46:39 PM

To: Santa Claus

Subject: Special Request

Dear Santa,

I'm writing to you tonight because I have a very special request. I know you are very busy getting ready for the big night and all, but I need you to visit my family in Hoytsville next Wednesday at 10:00 AM. My husband, Toby, and I have been foster parents for the past twelve years. We've had thirty-six children come through our home. We have five children of our own. Colton is twenty-two, Kyler is twenty, Rayli is seventeen, Ryden is fourteen, and Briel is ten. We adopted one of the foster children eight years ago; her name is Serenity, and she is now twelve years old. We are fostering a baby girl, Hayvin, fourteen months old. She came to our home when the authorities brought her to us in the middle of the night back in August when she had nowhere else to go. We have three foster children in our home who are originally from Mexico. Monica is fourteen, Alan is eleven, and Nate is eight. They lived with us for a couple of weeks about six years ago until the authorities located some family. But that was short lived, and they came back to live with us and have been here for five years now. These are amazing kids that have gone through so much, and we love them dearly!

All of the pieces of our family have miraculously come together, and we want you to deliver an important message to our family.

With love,
Natalie

It was a crisp December morning as I circled the village of Hoytsville, preparing to land. The landscape was frosted with fresh, fallen snow. Old farmhouses and beautiful custom cabin homes provided a picturesque view. My Elf Intel indicated that this little hamlet had a population of 524 souls. A dual stretch of road ran alongside each other through the narrow valley, with the Interstate separating them in the middle. The town itself was surrounded by mountains on either side. Six miles north, a smoky haze marked the town of Coalville, which seemed to be the center of commerce for this rural area.

My heart was racing with excitement at being a part of this family's big day and for the surprise we were about to reveal. I landed at the end of the long driveway that led up to the Kershaw home. The house was more contemporary than the surrounding neighbors. The exterior boasted rough-hewn wood beams that ran the circumference of the home and a stone façade punctuated by angular rock slabs that were probably quarried nearby.

As I walked up the driveway, the side door of the house opened and out came Natalie, Aunt Mandy, and Grandma Kathy. They were grinning from ear to ear. Natalie was all dressed up in a white blouse and mid-calf skirt. Mandy had a nice DSLR camera strapped around her neck. Grandma looked more like an older sister, rather than their mother. Each one of them gave me a big hug and truly made me feel welcomed. We huddled in the driveway as Natalie explained the plan.

"We've told everyone that we are taking family pictures today, that's why Toby, me, and all of the children are dressed up. We'll go in a little bit ahead of you and get everyone sitting in the living room. Then you come in and do your magic."

"Thank you for the invitation to be here. I'm honored to be a part of your special day. This is going to be memorable," I said.

The ladies disappeared into the house. I stepped up onto the landing outside of the side door. I paused. I took a deep breath in through my nose and exhaled through my mouth. I could see my breath against the backdrop of the pine trees in the distance. I closed my eyes for a moment to get a feel for the situation inside of the house. I sensed how important this day was to everyone involved. I was also prompted to enter the home with a more somber tone than I usually do when I bound into a home for a daylight visit. I turned the doorknob slowly and pushed the door open just a crack. I could hear bustling children's voices. I peeked through the crack. I could only see the empty kitchen in front of me. I stepped in and closed the door quietly behind me. I tiptoed through the kitchen to be as stealthy as possible. I was about halfway through the kitchen when one of the younger children squealed, "Santa, it's Santa!"

Everyone turned in my direction and let out a collective cheer of celebration, "Santa's here!" I stretched out my arms to invite the children to come to me. All the children rushed to greet me. They formed a huddle around me and then closed in. Even Colton joined in the group hug; he wasn't too old for Santa. Each of the boys wore white shirts, and the girls were wearing white dresses. It was then that I understood the theme of the family pictures Aunt Mandy had been taking before I arrived. I squeezed the hug tighter and could feel the tender goodness of these sweet children.

"Santa, come sit over here in this big chair," Toby requested. He was holding baby Hayvin. She looked like she could have been one of their biological children. She looked just like them.

The huddle broke. I walked toward the large, brown, leather chair Toby was directing me to. Then I stopped suddenly. I looked around the living room. A high vaulted ceiling rose to a point twenty feet high with rustic beams exposed. There was a large rock fireplace on the far side of the room. The mantle was decorated with two snowmen, a reindeer, a wooden letter "K," and a large, framed picture of Jesus teaching four small children. To the left of the fireplace was a large Christmas tree trimmed to perfection with red and gold ornaments, red ribbons, and tiny white lights. As I looked around the room, the children searched for what I was looking for. I looked behind the couch. I looked behind the drapes. I looked high and low.

"Where is he?"

"Where's who?" Briel asked.

"Murray, where's Murray? Is he hiding again, that little stinker? Murray, you can run, but you can't hide from old Santa."

The children rose to their feet and stretched out their arms, all pointing excitedly at the shelf above the mantle in the far corner of the room. I turned to look where they were all pointing.

"There he is, Santa. He's on the shelf."

I bounded toward the fireplace and stepped up on the hearth. I stretched up with my right arm and retrieved Murray, the Kershaw family's Elf on the Shelf.

"What in the world are you doing clear up there on that shelf, Murray?"

I brought Murray close to my face to make direct eye contact. The kids were laughing at the sight of me holding their little elf and treating him like a real person.

"No comment, huh? You get yourself into more trouble than any other elf on my team. Thank you, Murray, for watching over this wonderful family and reporting to me how they are doing this Christmas."

I pushed Murray's head forward with my right index finger to suggest that he was nodding yes to me. The room filled with laughter.

"What? What's that?" I asked Murray. I pulled his head to my left ear as though Murray was now whispering. "There's a puzzle in the room that we need to solve? Wait, what?" Murray whispered in my ear again. "Oh, I get it. Murray says there are nine pieces of paper hidden in this room. We need to find the pieces of paper and put them together as a puzzle to reveal a very special message for your family," I explained.

As though the starting pistol had just fired to start a race, the children began frantically searching the living room for the hidden pieces of the puzzle. The older kids were looking up high on shelves and behind decorations. The younger kids were looking under tables, couch cushions, and behind the lamps.

Ryden stood on a chair and waved a piece of the puzzle in the air. "I found one."

Everyone ran over to Ryden to look at the piece of the puzzle. It was a long, narrow strip of white paper with some red letters on it. The letters were cut off on the strip, so what you could read didn't make sense.

Then, Serenity squealed, "Me too, I found one too."

"You have found two pieces, we need to find seven more," I said with a sense of urgency in my voice.

The children's search became intensified. Natalie, Toby, Mandy, and Grandma Kathy watched the chaos from the sidelines. They were obviously amused by the looks on their faces.

"I found one over here," Rayli said from over near the kitchen.

Kyler shouted, "Look, there's one under the chair." He knelt down and retrieved it.

One by one, the children found each of the nine pieces of the puzzle. I sat down in the large, leather chair. "Let's put all of the puzzle pieces on the coffee table and see what the puzzle says."

The children bent close to the coffee table, eager to get as near as they could. Slowly, one at a time, the nine pieces of the puzzle were placed together. Some of the pieces were upside down. Colton took the lead and helped everyone make sure they were all turned in the same direction. Collectively, they moved the pieces around. The message still didn't make any sense. A feeling of anticipation built as some of the pieces began to fall into place.

"You are today getting become to and," Briel read out loud.

The pieces weren't in the right order. Natalie came over and peeked over their shoulders. You could cut the tension with a knife.

"What does it say, what does it say?" Serenity pleaded.

Monica was kneeling in front of the puzzle. She read it to herself and then put her hands on the side of her face. She stood up. She pressed her fingers into the corners of her eyes and wiped the tears down her cheeks. Alan and Nate both looked at Monica in unison to make sure their sister was all right.

"Rayli, why don't you read the puzzle out loud so all of us know what it says," I whispered.

Rayli leaned in closer to the puzzle and read the message, "Today you are getting adopted and going to the temple to become a forever family."

Alan and Nate looked at each other, processing the news. Monica looked up with tear-filled eyes. She looked over at Natalie. I had been so engrossed with all that was unfolding at the coffee table, I hadn't been paying attention to the grownups in the room. As Monica's gaze met Natalie's, the look on Monica's face intensified. She didn't need words. Natalie was crying tears of joy and mouthed the words "I love you" from across the room. Monica looked at Toby, Mandy, and Grandma Kathy. They didn't need verbal words to communicate what was in her heart.

I'd like to say that I was stoic in that moment to represent all of the strength of Santa, but I honestly couldn't speak.

My eyes were full of tears as I watched the kids embrace each other with unbridled joy. They all knew what Monica, Alan, and Nate had been through in their young lives: being bounced around between various family members, seeing their father deported, and not having any communication with their mother. I received a high-speed download of all the emotions Monica, Alan, and Nate were experiencing. The hugs turned into jumping around the room together, arm in arm.

Monica stood in the middle of her new brothers and sisters.

Her joy was radiant. She was laughing and crying at once. Her happiness was contagious. It spread to each of the children in the room. Monica's tear-soaked eyes were brighter than the lights on the Christmas tree; they were full of hope and joy. Usually during a Santa visit, we would sing some Christmas songs together. However, at that moment, I felt we should sing a different song together. I cleared my throat. I tried to speak. My voice cracked. Santa has a special gift to know the people he is visiting. He knows their language. He knows their traditions. He knows their culture. I felt prompted to sing a song that would be familiar to this family.

"Hmmmmm, we have a favorite song that comes from the Elf Songbook up at the North Pole. I know that you all know the song. I'll start singing it, and then you join in when you recognize the song," I explained with a definite quiver in my voice.

I began singing, *"I have a family here on earth ..."*

I lost it. I mean, I really lost it. A surge of joy and warmth coursed through my veins.

Everyone in the room knew the song; they picked up where I left off.

"... they are so good to me.

I want to share my life with them through all eternity. Families can be together forever through Heavenly Father's plan.

I always want to be with my own family, and the Lord has shown me how I can.

The Lord has shown me how I can."

(*Children's Songbook*, page 188, music and lyrics by Ruth Muir Gardner, 1927–1999. © 1980 IRI)

The entire room glowed with an increased tangible indescribable feeling of love and light. Monica walked over to me.

I wrapped my arms around her. She tucked her arms into my embrace. I just held her. I had learned that silence is best in these situations. People will forget the words we say, but they never forget the feelings they experience.

"Thank you, Santa," Monica said as she looked deep into my eyes. "For the last five years, all I have been asking for Christmas is a family, and this year I finally got one. This is my Christmas miracle."

Tears streamed down our faces, mixed with smiles so wide our cheeks ached. It was a moment of pure joy and love. Monica could hardly contain her happiness, beaming from ear to ear as she realized that her wish had finally come true—she had a family to call her own. Toby and Natalie were shedding tears of joy as they overheard what Monica was sharing with me. They knew firsthand the blood, sweat, and tears they had sacrificed to make her dream a reality. They had faced the odds, braved endless mountains of paperwork and legal hurdles, and paid the price to adopt these three beautiful children. But it was worth every sleepless night and stressful day just for this moment alone. And now, looking at that pure happiness on Monica's face, they knew without a shadow of a doubt that it had all been worth it.

Alan and Nate joined in on our hug. We held each other tight. I could only imagine what these three children had been through together. Monica released her embrace with me and walked around the room, hugging each member of her new family with all her might. She and her brothers had been part of the Kershaw family for years, but now they were going to be legally adopted, making their bond even stronger. With each hug, Monica's joyous laughter filled the air like music notes on a page, marking this momentous occasion in a way that words never could. As I watched her embrace her new siblings with an array of emotions passing over my face, I felt grateful to witness such an intimate moment through Santa's eyes.

I walked over and hugged Natalie and Toby to congratulate them for their hard work and sacrifice. Natalie told me the family was now heading to the Summit County courthouse where the judge would make the adoption legal. Then, they would conclude their day at their church where the children would be spiritually adopted.

I posed for family pictures, feeling so grateful to have been a part of this special moment. As they gathered around me, I couldn't help but notice the way they looked at each other— the pride Toby had for his children, the love and devotion Natalie had for her family, and the pure joy emanating from Monica, Alan, and Nate. It was a moment that will stay with me forever.

"Beautiful, I think we got some good pictures," Mandy said as she put down her camera.

I stepped over by the Christmas tree and said, "Group hug!"

All nine of the children put their arms on each other's shoulders and leaned into the middle of the circle.

"I love you all. Merry Christmas," I whispered.

"Merry Christmas, Santa. We love you," they said as one voice.

We said our goodbyes. Grandma walked me through the kitchen to the door. She gave me a big hug.

"Thank you for making today so special, Santa."

"Thank you for asking me to be a part of this celebration. I will always cherish this visit."

As I climbed back into my sleigh, I couldn't help but reflect on the miracle I had witnessed through Santa's eyes. The love and joy that had permeated every corner of the room filled me with a warmth that I knew would stay with me for a long time. I snapped the reins, and my trusty reindeer took off into the sky, the magic of Christmas propelling us forward toward our next destination.

As we flew over the rooftops, I couldn't help but think about all the families out there who were still waiting for their own Christmas miracle. So many children who longed for a home and a family to call their own. I vowed in that moment to do everything in my power to make their dreams come true, just as we had done for Monica, Alan, and Nate.

~ 7 ~

You Are My Sunshine

Christmas, my child, is love in action.
Every time we love, every time we give, it's Christmas.

– DALE EVANS

THE AIR WAS ELECTRIC with anticipation as Christmas Eve drew near, the night where I'd circle the globe delivering love to everyone. I was working alongside Tyler, Ben, and Mark—my top three elves—when Mrs. Claus burst through the workshop door.

"Santa," she said, nearly out of breath, "you must prepare the sleigh at once and fly to Cottonwood Heights for a special breakfast for the Gibbs family Christmas party. The elves have crafted some special gifts that must be delivered right now. Hurry, don't be late."

I was surprised, but I didn't question Mrs. Claus. She always knows best, and when she tells me to do something right now, I know it must be important. I instructed my elves to load the sleigh while I donned my red coat and prepared for the flight.

As I climbed into my sleigh, I could feel that today would be a particularly special day. I knew that something magical was about to happen. Flying over the snow-capped Rocky Mountains, I couldn't help but wonder what gifts my elves had crafted for the Gibbs family.

As we landed on the snow-covered front lawn, I took in a deep breath, taking in the scent of cinnamon rolls and hot chocolate wafting through the air.

I sneaked up to the front door and peeked through the little window. The large family was gathered in the living room. There were several large tables pushed together to make one long table that filled the entire room. The room was packed wall-to-wall with aunts and uncles, nieces and nephews, and cousins. I could hear laughter and the sounds of a happy family sharing fun conversations. As soon as I saw all of those plates of delicious food, the decorations, and everyone wearing their new pajamas, I knew this event for this family was something special; it was a celebration and a reunion.

I opened the front door and sailed into the living room. "Ho, Ho, Ho!" I exclaimed with great excitement.

The room went completely silent. Everyone looked stunned.

"Wow, tough crowd," I said.

The Gibbs family was completely taken by surprise. All eyes were on me. They weren't expecting a visit from me because it wasn't Christmas yet.

Once the family processed what was happening, they snapped back into consciousness and began cheering and clapping.

"Yeah, Santa is here," yelled fourteen-year-old Cody as he hurdled the furniture to greet me with a huge bear hug.

"Now, that is more like it. Who is excited for Christmas?"

"We are, Santa!"

I made my way around the room, shaking hands, giving high-fives and knuckles to everyone. I could tell that this family had a lot of love in their hearts for each other. When you have your heart open, you can feel it the moment you walk into a room. I climbed over children, toys, and furniture to complete my opening greetings. When I got to the back of the living room, I realized the family was also spread out into the kitchen area.

Sue got my attention from across the room. "Santa, come over here," she said.

I climbed back over everybody to a clearing at the head of the long table.

"We are really excited to have Santa Claus join us for our family breakfast today. This is a very special time of the year for our family," Sue said.

"I'm honored you invited me to join your family breakfast, you've made me feel very welcome. I'd like to think I'm an honorary Gibbs now," I said.

"Yes, you are, Santa," Sue agreed.

"I was working in my workshop this morning at the North Pole when Mrs. Claus informed me that I had to get here at once to deliver some special gifts early. Would it be all right if I deliver some gifts before Christmas?"

"Yes, Santa," everyone agreed.

"You know, I have been working so hard at the North Pole that I haven't had time to stop and feel the spirit of Christmas like I usually do. There is one thing that makes me feel the spirit of Christmas and that is hearing families sing Christmas songs. Let's sing some Christmas songs together!"

The Gibbs family hooted and hollered, "We love Christmas songs, Santa."

Some families sound like beautiful choirs when they sing, others not so much. I would give the Gibbs family an A for effort. What they lacked in harmony, they made up for with unbridled energy. I laughed out loud at the way they delivered their renditions of the Christmas classics. I always enjoy my visits to families, but I bonded instantly with this family. There was a strong feeling of unity and love here. I knew someone was the uniter of this family; someone was the glue that held this crew together.

After the sing-along concluded, I reached down and slid my big, red bag next to me. I untied the gold rope that held it closed. I opened the bag; it was full of gifts that were all the same size. Each one was a square box wrapped in identical paper. In most cases I deliver a variety of presents of different sizes, shapes, and colors. There was a piece of paper folded in half resting on top of the presents. I felt impressed to have someone read what was on the paper.

I looked around the room, searching for the person who was supposed to read it. Then my eyes connected with a woman standing near the back of the living room.

I extended my arm and motioned for the woman to join me. She pointed to herself, questioning if I meant her.

"Yes, you, please join me up here," I said.

The room broke out with a cheer. "Yeah, Mary, you get to help Santa."

Mary joined me in front of the family. She looked a little nervous about what was happening. Honestly, I didn't know what was happening either. When you're prompted to do something, you go with it. I handed the piece of paper to Mary. She unfolded it and began reading it to herself. Her countenance changed. She looked over at Sue with tears in her eyes.

"This is the poem our mom wrote a few years ago after she had attended a Christmas program that meant so much to her," Mary explained.

Mary turned to me and shared that her mother, Patti, had passed away about five years ago. She told me how her mother loved Christmas and how much this family meant to her. I knew at that moment it was Patti who was the uniter of this family; Patti was the special glue that sealed this family together.

Mary cleared her throat and read the poem aloud:

My Carol,

it's Christmas time again.

That crazy time of year.

We are running to and fro

in search of Christmas cheer.

It isn't really there,

in all the gifts and trees,

not in the twinkling lights;

it's nothing you can see.

But when the music of the Christ child

fills my troubled mind,

the Spirit gently tells me that

He really was divine.

I know my Savior lived

so many years ago.

He taught and loved and healed,

wherever He would go.

His love can never die.

Of such there is no end.

To us He freely gives.

He truly is our friend.

So when I think of Christmas
and the search for gifts and cheer,
it really is the gift of love
we give throughout the year.
Accept this gift of love
that money cannot buy.
Give as He would have given
and keep His love alive.

– Patti Weighall

As Mary concluded the poem, I looked around the room. All of the grownups had tears in their eyes. I sensed the power these words had in their hearts. I knew what Patti meant to all of them. The children were completely quiet and honored what Mary shared.

"Why did you have me read that poem?" Mary asked.

"I just felt you were the one that was supposed to," I said.

Mary folded the paper and gave me a big hug.

"Thank you, Santa," Mary said softly in my ear.

I reached down and retrieved one of the gifts from my bag and handed it to Mary.

"The elves at the North Pole have hand-crafted a special gift for each of you, identical to what Mary is holding. Mary, why don't you unwrap your present so we can all see what everyone is receiving," I proposed.

Mary sat the poem on a chair beside her. She began to unwrap the gift. I held onto the wrapping paper while she pulled out a white box. She opened the lid to reveal a beautiful, wooden music box that she held up so everyone could see. There were several whispers of approval from the adults, but I could not make out what they said. The inside of the lid contained an image of Patti, and her beaming face showed how special she was; I felt the warmth radiating from her goodness. As soon as Mary opened the music box, the tune of "You Are My Sunshine" started playing. The melody filled the room with an incredible energy of peace and love.

When the tune concluded, Mary explained to me how Patti had used this song for so long to bring comfort and love to each of her children and grandchildren. Every night before bed, Patti would sing "You Are My Sunshine" to each of them. Mary also told me that Patti had recorded her singing the song on the phone app Marco Polo, allowing even those far away from her to feel the comforting embrace of this beloved melody. Patti kept singing the song until her death, wanting to make sure every single one of them knew they were loved just as much as the day before.

The music box was a reminder that no matter how far apart they were, this family was connected through Patti's love; it was a reminder to all of the Gibbs family what it meant to be connected; it transcended time and space and served as a unifying force among this tightly knit family. We all felt deeply honored by Patti's gesture; if anyone needed tangible evidence of their mother's everlasting presence in their lives, here it was. The music box embodied everything that made Patti amazing, her ever-present love and kindness that acted as the special glue that sealed this family together.

I stood ready as Mary took out each of the presents from my bag and presented them to everyone in the family. Everyone embraced her in gratitude as they received their gift.

I asked Mary if there was anything else I could do for them to mark this special occasion. "We just want to take the time to honor our mom today," Mary said, looking around the room at her siblings and their families.

In honor of Patti and her love, we concluded our time together with a new Christmas song. I suggested that it become a new family tradition to sing "You Are My Sunshine" every year for Christmas in remembrance of Patti's loving presence in all of their lives. Together, we all sang "You Are My Sunshine." It echoed off the walls, its beautiful melody ringing through each corner of the room like an inspirational prayer meant to carry us all high into the atmosphere above us. There was a tangible feeling of love. As we finished off this timeless classic about sunshine and happiness, it felt like Patti herself had wrapped us up snugly in her warm embrace one last time, reminding us why Christmas is such an incredibly special time for this family.

I finished off my time in the Gibbs home with a group hug with all of the children. I made my way around the room sharing hugs with all of the grownups too. Sue handed a plate of goodies to her children, Addie and Camden, and had them walk me to the door.

"Merry Christmas, Santa," Addie and Camden said, their eyes sparkling with the magic and joy of Christmas.

As I stepped outside into the snow-covered morning and began my journey back to the workshop, I knew I had been a part of something truly incredible. The love contained in that small music box reminded me of everything special about Christmas: family, connection, love, and peace. It filled my heart with warmth as I flew away back to the North Pole feeling blessed to have been a part of this unforgettable family experience.

8

The Envelope

Blessed is the season which engages the whole world
in a conspiracy of love.

– Hamilton Wright Mabie

"Hi, this is Santa. What kind of magic can we share tonight?" I said, answering the phone.

"Santa, my name is Steve. My family needs your help. We need you to make a special delivery for us tonight. We want to help a family across town, but we don't want them to know who is doing it. Can you stop by our house and pick up an envelope then deliver it to a family for us?"

"I'd be happy to make a special Christmas delivery," I said.

Steve gave me his address, and I plugged in the coordinates to my Elf GPS on the sleigh. In an instant, we arrived at Steve's house. The home was decorated with an amazing show of Christmas lights, and trees adorned the wrap-around porch, all designed according to a unique theme.

I rapped on the door, and Steve opened it. Wendy, his wife, was standing next to him along with their four children, Dan, Travis, Teresa, and Jana.

"C'mon in, Santa," Steve invited.

"We'd like to share Christmas with some other family, but we want it to remain anonymous," Wendy said.

"Tell me a little bit more about the family," I inquired.

Wendy explained, "The family has four children. Two of the kids have special needs and a lot of medical bills. Jessica is a single mother, working long hours to raise all of them. Her life is difficult, and she barely gets by every month. Our family has more than enough, and we want to share to bless their family this Christmas."

"I've grown close to Candice, one of the girls with special needs. She is the most generous and gentle person I've ever met. So, I asked my parents if our family could help her family this Christmas. My dad and mom agreed to donate," Jana explained.

Jana handed me a red envelope, which certainly contained a Christmas card, but when I held it, the envelope felt like it contained more than just a card. I sensed it contained a stack of cash.

I secured the envelope inside my thick, black belt.

"You, my friends, are being elfish to bless the lives of another family for Christmas. God bless you for your efforts. May you have a very Merry Christmas and know that your gift will be received with love," I said.

I thanked the family for the opportunity to be the messenger to deliver their gift of love and service.

I flew across the valley and landed outside of a small, red, brick house. The home's exterior had no lights or decorations, leaving it unremarkable compared to its festive neighbors. I made my way around to the side of the house and descended the narrow, concrete stairs leading to the basement entrance where the family resided.

With a steady knock on the door, I waited patiently for an answer. Finally, after what felt like an eternity, teenage girl answered the door. Her eyes widened in shock at the sight of me standing at the door. She let out a piercing scream that echoed through the quiet neighborhood. "Santa, what are you doing here? Christmas isn't for a few more days."

"I have a special delivery for Candice and her family," I said.

"Candice is my sister. My name is Laura. She and the rest of my family are upstairs visiting the old lady that rents the basement to us," she explained.

"C'mon, Laura, let's go upstairs together and deliver a special gift to Candice and your family."

Laura bolted past me and headed up the stairs for the front door of the house. I had to run to catch up. Laura swung the front door wide open and yelled, "Look everybody, Santa is here for Candice."

The family were all sitting in the living room visiting with an elderly woman. One of the teenage girls jumped up from the couch. "I'm Candice, I'm Candice," she exclaimed.

"Of course, I know you, Candice. May I come in and share a few minutes with all of you?"

The elderly woman greeted me with a warm smile and gestured for me to join her near the modestly decorated Christmas tree, offering me the comfortable recliner.

"Welcome to my home, Santa. I'm Marilyn," she said.

"Merry Christmas, Marilyn. Thank you for the warm welcome," I said.

"What brings you out on such a cold night, Santa?" Marilyn asked.

"I'm here to make a special Christmas delivery. I know it's a few days before Christmas, but I wanted you to have it before the big day."

Candice was bouncing up and down. "You brought us presents, Santa? Yippie!"

"I brought you an envelope that contains many gifts. But before I leave it, I want to know who everybody is," I explained.

The people in the room all introduced themselves, one after the other. Jessica, who sat at the end of the couch, declared she was a mother to the "yahoos" around her. Nothing escaped my notice; I saw how haggard and tired she looked and noted her missing teeth on the top row of her smile and only a few left on the bottom. She wore clothes that had been through better days and sneakers with holes in them. I understood in an instant that this woman had made great sacrifices for her children.

"Jessica, you have a beautiful family, and I can tell how much you love them," I said.

Candice came over and sat on my left knee and put her right arm around my neck. She leaned in almost nose to nose. She just stared at me with a look of disbelief. "Are you the real Santa Claus?" she asked.

"Yes, I am," I said.

"Prove it to me," Candice demanded.

"Well, the reindeer are down the street sharing a bale of hay and don't like to be disturbed while they are eating, so I won't show you them tonight. But I happen to know something about you, Candice. I know what your favorite thing about Christmas is ..."

"My favorite thing about Christmas is giving presents to my family," Candice finished my sentence for me.

"Yes, that's just what I was about to say."

"I love getting my family presents and seeing the look on their faces when they get something really special that they wanted. I love to give," Candice said.

"Good for you. That's what Christmas is all about. We call that being elfish at the North Pole," I said.

"Elfish, what does that mean?" Candice asked.

"It's the opposite of being selfish. Selfish is when we think only about ourselves. Being elfish means we think about others first," I explained.

"I like being elfish," Candice said with wide eyes and a big smile.

"I can tell you're very elfish, Candice."

Candice giggled.

"When we go to the store for just normal things and we don't have enough money for even all the groceries we need, well, we have to put some of it back. So, I take pictures of everything. And I put them in a folder on my phone, so that if I ever have any money, I would be able to get those things for my family," Candice explained.

I said, "Well, what kinds of things are in your folder?"

Candice pulled out a well-used smartphone from her pocket. The screen was shattered but she didn't seem to mind. She opened up her pictures app and showed me a folder she had created titled "Family."

"If I had any money, I would buy my family the things in this folder," Candice said. She showed me pictures she had taken with her phone: a loaf of bread, a gallon of milk, a carton of eggs, a box of cereal, and a few other basic groceries. Then she said, "Well, if I really could get what was in my folder, I'd get this for my brother, and this for my sister. But the thing I would get for my brother is just way too expensive."

I said, "Whoa, how much would that be?"

Candice said, "Santa, something like that would be like ten dollars."

Then I said, "What do you think it would cost to buy everything in that folder that your family really needs and some little extras that they might want?"

"Oh, Santa. That would be a lot of money. That would be like ..." Candice paused and looked at the ceiling like she was using a big calculator. "It would be like two hundred dollars!" she said as though two hundred dollars might as well be one million dollars.

"Candice, I want to give you and your family everything in that folder for Christmas," I said.

"No way, Santa. That would be impossible," Candice challenged.

I reached into my belt and pulled out the envelope. Candice attempted to grab it out of my hand.

"Why don't we have Mom help you open it?" I offered.

Jessica got off of the couch and kneeled by Candice. She helped Candice open the envelope. I didn't want Candice to pull out all of the cash in front of everyone, so I helped too. I held the envelope open so Jessica could see what was inside. Candice put her finger in the envelope and fanned through the stack of hundred-dollar bills. Even I was taken back by the generosity of the gift in the envelope. I imagined there was enough money for several months of rent, a car payment or two, and plenty of money for a good Christmas.

Jessica gasped and covered her mouth with her hands. "Oh, dear!" She sighed. She looked up at me and said, "Thank you, Santa. Thank you, Santa."

"I'm just the delivery person tonight. I couldn't do amazing things like this without the help of special elves who love you and care about you," I said.

"Who did this?" Jessica pleaded.

"My elves wish to remain anonymous. That's what being elf-ish is all about," I explained.

Candice jumped off my knee and bounced around the room.

"I need to thank the person who did this," Jessica said.

"This a gift from an entire family who loves you and wants you to have a Merry Christmas," I said.

I had an idea. All too often my elves who make these kinds of Christmas miracles a reality don't get to see the lives they impact.

"Jessica, I'll let you thank my elves who did this while keeping who they are a secret."

I stood up and pulled my phone out of my pocket. I opened the camera app and set it to video mode. Jessica stood by my side as I recorded both of us.

"Hello, secret Santa family. I'm here with Jessica, Candice, and the rest of the family. They want to share a message with you," I said.

"I don't know who you are, but you have answered my prayers and given my family a Christmas miracle. I can't tell you how much your generous gift means to all of us," Jessica said.

Candice jumped into the video and said, "Merry Christmas, elves, we love you."

I ended the recording.

"I promise I'll send the video to the good people responsible for blessing your family tonight," I said.

I shared a few more minutes with Jessica and her family. They took a ton of pictures. I had no doubt all of these pictures would end up in a folder on Candice's phone.

I ended the visit with all of us singing "We Wish You a Merry Christmas."

Marilyn walked me to the door and gave me a big hug.

"Thank you, Santa. Seeing what happened here tonight made this a very special Christmas for me too."

I hugged Marilyn back and thanked her from the bottom of my heart for all she was doing to help Jessica and her family.

"It's people like you, Marilyn, who make Christmas a time for giving, not just receiving," I said warmly. "Your selflessness and generosity is an inspiration to Jessica and to me."

Marilyn stood in the doorway as I made my way to the sleigh. I grinned as I climbed into the sleigh, grateful to Steve and Wendy for making sure Jessica's family would have an unforgettable Christmas. I blew Marilyn a kiss goodbye before heading off into the night sky illuminated by millions of twinkling stars that lit up the world below.

~ 9 ~

Santa's Angels

When we remember a special Christmas, it is not
the presents that made it special, but the laughter,
the feeling of love, and the togetherness of friends
and family that made that Christmas special.

– CATHERINE PULSIFER

IT WAS CHRISTMAS EVE EVE, the night before Christmas Eve, and I was sitting at my desk in the workshop at the North Pole checking the "Nice List" one last time to make sure I had everything right when the phone rang. I removed my spectacles and placed them on the desk. It was a pediatrician named Dr. Mark Brown calling with an urgent request.

Dr. Brown explained that he had a six-year-old patient named Jacob who was dying of leukemia. Dr. Brown didn't expect him to live much longer. Dr. Brown told me that Jacob's final wish was to receive a visit from Santa Claus before he went back to Heaven. My heart sank at the thought of such a young boy facing such a challenge as this. Even though Christmas can be the happiest time of the year, it can also be filled with difficulties and tough times. It is situations like this that I am reminded of my mission; to bless the lives of children of all ages and make their Christmas wishes come true. I grabbed a wrapped present off the workbench and placed it in my bag. I was off to a city called West Jordan, where I would visit Jacob at his home.

When I arrived at Jacob's house, his mother, Lori, welcomed me at the front door. She had a look of concern on her face.

"Thank you for coming to our home, Santa. I know how busy you are getting ready for the big night. My little Jacob said he just had to see you. I told Dr. Brown I didn't know what to do. Dr. Brown said he would make a call, and here you are," Lori said.

"Dr. Brown and I go way back to when he was Jacob's age," I said with a wink.

Lori led me to Jacob's bedroom. She stood outside of the room as I slowly peeked my head around the corner. Jacob was lying in his bed with his covers pulled up to his chin. His eyes were closed.

Jacob's room was perfectly decorated with all of the superheroes. His dresser was lined with all of the figurines, like Spiderman, Batman and Robin, Captain America, and some I didn't recognize. There was a big poster of Superman hanging over his bed. Instrumental Christmas music was playing softly from a small speaker on the nightstand.

Lori stepped into the doorway and looked at Jacob. "He drifts in and out because of the medicine he's on," Lori said.

"I understand," I said as quietly as possible, trying not to wake Jacob.

Jacob was pale, and his eyes were sunken. I couldn't even imagine what this sweet, little boy had been through in his short few years on earth. I stepped slowly toward his bed. As I went to sit in the chair beside his bed, Jacob opened up his eyes a bit. His eyelids fluttered like the wings of a butterfly attempting to take flight. I stopped in my tracks. When he saw it was me, his eyes opened wider, and he struggled to give me a smile. I knelt by his bed.

"Hi, buddy. It's me, Santa," I whispered.

Jacob's smile became a bit wider and stronger.

"Hi, Santa. I just knew you'd come. I just knew it," Jacob whispered slowly and so softly I leaned it to make sure I could hear him.

"I wouldn't miss our visit for the world. There isn't anywhere in the world I would rather be than right here with you," I said.

"Is it Christmas Eve?" Jacob asked.

I turned at looked at Lori still standing in the doorway. I gestured for her to come sit in the chair next to Jacob's bed. Lori sat next to us on the chair.

"Almost, buddy. Tonight is Christmas Eve Eve. That's what the elves and I call it at the North Pole. It's the night before Christmas Eve," I said.

"How are the elves doing?" Jacob asked softly.

"Oh, they are so good. I have the best elves on the planet. Well, except for my elf, Ben. He can be quite a character, you know," I struggled to say, trying to be a little funny but fighting back the emotions that were percolating inside of me.

Jacob grinned. "How's Rudolph?" he then asked.

"Rudy is good. You might as well know we call him Rudy for short at the North Pole. Only special people know that secret," I said.

"Is Rudy here?" asked Jacob.

"Yes, he's down in the park at the end of your street. I think he's playing some reindeer games with the rest of the team. Old Rudy keeps me on my toes," I said.

Jacob shared a soft giggle with me.

"It is very kind of you to ask about the elves and the reindeer. How are you?" I asked.

"I'm good, Santa. I hurt a lot, and my doctor gives me medicine to make me better. I was in the hospital. He let me come home for Christmas," Jacob said.

I looked over at Lori. She looked away, trying to conceal her tears. I placed my hand on hers and gave a slight squeeze. She looked back at me with an expression of gratitude, tears streaming down her cheeks.

Jacob slowly pulled his hand from underneath the covers and reached out to touch my cheek. I leaned in to meet him halfway.

"You are real," Jacob sighed.

"Yes, I am Santa."

Jacob looked deep into my eyes. I looked deep into his eyes. I can't describe in words the special connection we made. I can only explain it as divine, not of this world. My heart surged with pure love for this sweet, little boy lying here helpless but with so much belief, so much hope. I struggled for something to say. What could I say at this moment? I said a silent prayer for God to put some words in my mouth.

"I love you, Jacob," I said. "Mrs. Claus, all of the elves, and all of the reindeer love you so much. And we are so proud of you for being such a special boy and being so strong. You are my Superman, like the one on your wall."

"Thanks, Santa," Jacob said. "Tell me what it's like to be Santa."

I shared with Jacob a few stories about visiting children around the world. I told him about the snow-covered forests and majestic peaks I had flown over on my travels. I told him about making deliveries on Christmas Eve. Jacob just kept looking deep into my eyes.

"My favorite thing about being Santa is sharing time with special little people like you," I said with a sniffle, trying to keep my nose from running.

Jacob strained to look over at his mom. She smiled back at him with such love in her heart, you could feel it.

"I brought you a present, buddy. Maybe Mom can help you open it," I said.

I reached into my bag that was sitting on the floor. I handed the gift to Lori. She set it on the bed by Jacob's hand and tore the wrapping paper a bit.

"I wonder what the elves wrapped up for you," I said.

Lori ripped the wrapping paper more and exposed the head of a small Teddy Bear.

"Wow, look at that. It's Ted E. Bear. Only the best little boys get that special gift," I said, making it up as I went.

Jacob pursed his lips and nodded. His eyes began fluttering again like he was just too tired to keep them open.

I removed the rest of the wrapping paper from the Teddy Bear and tucked it under the covers next to Jacob. I patted the bear's forehead.

I leaned in and whispered softly in Jacob's ear, "Remember, we all love you. Merry Christmas, little buddy."

Jacob slightly bit his lower lip but kept his grin. He closed his eyes.

Lori put her hand on my shoulder. I turned and looked at her, not knowing what to expect.

"He's just sleeping now. I know he's very happy you came to visit," Lori said.

I watched Jacob sleep for a few moments. He looked like a beautiful angel. I said another little silent prayer, thanking God for allowing me to be a part of this tender, precious moment. I felt comforted knowing this sweet, little boy was in God's care.

I kissed my middle and index finger and then touched them on Jacob's forehead.

I stood up and looked one last time at Jacob. I turned to leave the room, but Lori stopped me and buried her head in my beard.

"I'm not ready to say goodbye to my boy," she sobbed. "I'm not ready!"

I held her for a moment and patted her softly on the back. There was no way I could understand what she was going through.

Lori walked me to the front door. "Thank you, Santa, I can't thank you enough," she said in a strained, broken voice.

"We love you. God bless you," I said and turned to walk down the driveway. About halfway down the driveway, I turned and looked back at Lori. She waved goodbye with her fingertips and closed the door.

The next morning, I received a call from Lori to inform me that Jacob had passed away during the night. She told me that she was sleeping in his bed with him when she heard him whispering in the middle of the night. She asked Jacob who he was talking to. Jacob told her, "Santa's angels are here, and they're saying it's okay to go home, Mommy."

"With that, he closed his eyes and peacefully slipped into the arms of Jesus," Lori concluded.

I hung up the phone, my heart forever softened by my sweet little friend, Jacob.

~ 10 ~

Quiet Giving

The best of all gifts around any Christmas tree:
the presence of a happy family all wrapped up in each other.

– BURTON HILLS

CHRISTMAS EVE is an explosion of light, movement, and sound at the North Pole. An army of elves run from workshop to workshop with toy bags over their shoulders, hauling gifts out to my sleigh. Mrs. Claus inspects my appearance to make sure I look just right; my moustache is waxed, my warm overcoat is freshly brushed, and my boots are so shiny you can see the stars' reflection in them.

My head elf Ben stood waiting impatiently for me to climb into my sleigh.

"Santa, before you head southeast to Dublin to start your deliveries where all of the good Irish boys and girls are fast asleep, I need you to make one last in-person visit to a special family in the village of Willow Creek. They have a family Christmas party at Grandma Turley's before they all go home for the night," Ben barked the last-minute instructions.

"Aye, aye, captain," I said sarcastically as I gave him a big salute.

I flew south toward Utah and the snow-capped mountains. As I came on final approach to the village of Willow Creek, there was a glow of lights that spread out across the valley below. I checked my GPS to make sure I was landing at the right house. I picked out a landing area in the middle of the thick, evergreen forest.

As I circled the house, I could see the Turley family outside bundled in their coats and hats surrounding a large firepit in the backyard.

I landed without detection between the trees. The family was sitting by the fire. They were singing, "Here Comes Santa Claus," so I thought this was the perfect introduction. As they concluded with, "So let's give thanks to the Lord above, 'cause Santa Claus comes tonight," I magically appeared, standing right beside Grandma Turley's son-in-law, Carl. He turned and nearly jumped out of his shoes when he saw me.

"Santa, you nearly scared me to death. Don't sneak up like that. It's dark out here," Carl said, panting to catch his breath.

"M-e-r-r-y C-h-r-i-s-t-m-a-s, Turley family," I proclaimed in my most festive late-night TV host voice. "I was just about to start my deliveries in Ireland when my head elf Ben told me I needed to catch this family at your annual shindig before you all go home and go to bed."

Kalei, Grandma Turley's daughter, said, "That's right, Santa, we can't have a party without you."

I stepped in front of Carl and gave Kalei knuckles.

"Is she with you?" I asked Carl.

"Yes, she is my wife," Carl replied.

"Wow, you married out of your league," I said with a smile.

Everyone around the fire laughed, knowing that I was right on the mark with that comment.

Grandma Turley invited me to come around to the other side of the firepit and stand by her.

"I heard y'all singing as I landed. All my life I wished that I could sing, now I wish y'all could," I joked. I sensed this was a fun-loving family, but I had to test the waters to make sure. They all played along and dished right back.

Once we exchanged a heaping portion of friendly banter, I paused and changed the mood.

"Harold and Elaine Turley are well-known to all of us at the North Pole. The rest of the world might not know who they are because they are what we call 'quiet givers.' They are the perfect example of what it means to BE ELFISH. They serve and give like few ever do without any fanfare or desire for public recognition. So, tonight I would like to honor Harold, who is watching tonight from heaven, and his beautiful wife Elaine for their lifelong commitment to elfish service," I said proudly.

"Oh, Santa, we never did it for any recognition," Grandma Turley said with sincere humility.

"I know that, dear. That's why what you and your husband have done throughout your lives is remarkable. Too many people do service and then post pictures on social media bragging about what they've done. Is that elfish? I don't think so. Being elfish means in most cases that you do it anonymously, not seeking any recognition. You do it because you love people and want to serve them," I said.

"I remember when my dad passed away," Kalei began. "Strangers came up to me at his funeral and told me stories about how my dad paid for their college, bought the single mother a new car, and donated to missions around the world."

One by one, members of the family went around the circle

and recounted stories of how Harold and Elaine had quietly given to countless charities, foundations, missions, and causes around the world over the years. Grandma Turley sat quietly as everyone shared their stories.

"As you all know, I don't ask you what you want for Christmas. I ask you what you're going to give for Christmas," I said.

I reached into my bag and pulled out a stack of 4' X 6' laminated cards.

"Grandma Turley gets it! In her spirit of quiet giving, she has already given your gifts for you. When I call your name, come up here and stand next to me. I'm going to tell you what you gave for Christmas," I instructed.

All eyes were on me. As I read the cards, the family members mentioned came up and received the card of what they gave:

"Kathryn Turley-Sonne family, given by Elizabeth Sonne who understands the importance of this special cause. You are supporting the Circle of Friends Foundation. This organization helps communities be inclusive of the disabled by creating shared experiences that foster friendships."

"Kalei Turley-Budge family, given by Johnny and Kasdyn, you are giving new mother and baby kits to the less fortunate in Haiti. They just had a new baby and want to help new mothers and babies in the world."

"Trey Turley family, given by Dru Turley, you are giving to the Thailand Refugees in Salt Lake City because you served in Thailand."

"Susan Turley-Steiner family, given by Sydney to provide feminine hygiene kits for girls in Kenya."

"Derek Turley family, given by Rhett to the Orange Couch Foundation because she did a humanitarian trip to Guatemala. This foundation helps Guatemalan children receive a formal education."

One at a time, I went through every member of Grandma Turley's family and shared with the group what each of them had given, not received, for Christmas: piglets in Africa, chickens in Mexico, pre-natal care for expectant mothers in a third-world country, meals for the homeless in Boston, clothes for the underprivileged, school supplies for the less fortunate.

After I handed out all of the cards of their gifts, I put my hands together and applauded each of them for their gifts of service. "I applaud you and honor each of you," I said.

"Well done. That's what it means to be elfish. Now, will you join the movement to be more elfish? Invite all of your family and friends to take a portion of what they would spend on Christmas gifts and donate that money on behalf of the person they would be giving the present to. There are countless websites of charities, foundations, and worthy causes where you can donate on behalf of another person. Will you join the movement?"

"Yes," they all cheered.

I paused, went around the large circle, and looked into the eyes of each member of the Turley family.

A gentle breeze blew through the spruces in the background. The fire roared with increased intensity. A warm, peaceful feeling surrounded us.

"Can you feel that? What is that?" I asked.

I looked around the family. Then I looked at Grandma Turley. "What am I feeling?" I asked.

"I can feel my husband, Harold. He's here with us right now," Grandma Turley said.

You could hear sniffles and deep breaths.

Carl broke the silence. "I recognize the spirit of God is here with our family tonight. Can you all feel it?"

"Yes," a number of them responded.

"Look around this fire tonight. Remember the people here and what we are feeling. I promise all of you that years from now you will forget what you got for Christmas, but you will never forget who is here and what you're feeling. This is pure love," Carl declared.

"Amen," I whispered.

"Amen," the family said in unison.

I looked at my watch. "Wow, I gotta go. Join me for the grand finale, 'We Wish You a Merry Christmas.'"

The entire family stood and sang a hearty rendition of the song. It was spectacular; they meant every word.

And, as quickly as I had arrived, I disappeared into the night sky. From high above the trees, I proclaimed, "Merry Christmas to all, and to all a good night!"

~ 11 ~

The Proposal

*One of the most glorious messes in the world is the mess
created in the living room on Christmas Day.
Don't clean it up too quickly.*

– ANDY ROONEY

THE SPEED at which the reindeer and I travel on Christmas
Eve is truly a sight to behold. However, the way in which
we travel cannot be seen by human eyes. It's taken hundreds of
years to perfect the technology at the North Pole to stay ahead
of what mere mortals have in their world.

My delivery stops at each home around the world are so fast
and stealthy, the only way to understand it is to surrender traditional beliefs and know that there are invisible powers and
forces that make the magic of Christmas Eve travel possible.

Having made my deliveries in the Eastern and Midwestern
parts of North America, I was now heading west. By the time I
got to Riverton, a small town nestled between mountain ranges
close to the Rockies, I was running at a mad pace to stay on

time. Every year, more families and people are added to my annual route.

I rushed through each of the homes along Cottonwood Avenue and arrived at a large, rustic-looking abode at the end of the street, only to witness someone move swiftly past the front window. I ducked below the windowsill so they wouldn't see me. There was no time for any delays; I must be in and out in a flash. I slowly stood up to peek in the window. My breath fogged the glass, so I rubbed my hand on the window so I could see inside the house. The silhouette of a person darted across the room. I sneaked around to the side of the house to find another way in—dagnabit, the side door was locked. I skirted around to the back of the house. Yes! The back sliding door was unlocked.

I carefully tiptoed through the kitchen and into the living room, which was pitch black without the Christmas tree lights to illuminate it. Usually, people leave them on so I have enough light to work. I tripped over an ottoman and fell flat on my face. A hearty, masculine chuckle reverberated in the darkness, mocking me.

I rose to me knees, still ducking behind the ottoman.

"Who's there?" I asked.

"It's me, Reed," the man said from somewhere in the room.

"Reed, what are you doing up? Everyone is supposed to be asleep on Christmas Eve so you don't see me," I insisted with a stern whisper. "You know the rules."

"I'm waiting for you. I need your help to deliver my Christmas present to Stephanie," Reed said.

"Look, I have a schedule to keep. I gotta be quick here," I said.

The lights on the Christmas tree turned on, and the room was illuminated by the colorful glow. Reed was a handsome, muscular man with a trimmed full beard of brown hair. He was sitting on the couch across the room with his legs kicked up and crossed on the couch beside him. He was wearing red, plaid pajamas and heavy, wool socks.

"Don't you look cute," I said in a rather snarky tone.

"Well, thank you, Santa," Reed played back with me.

"How can I help you deliver your present?" I asked.

"You know that Stephanie and I have been dating for almost two years now?"

"Yes, congratulations!"

"Tonight, I need your help to ask her to marry me," Reed explained.

"Awe, isn't that's sweet, Reed. What if she doesn't say yes?"

"You're funny, Santa."

"Yes I am, Reed."

"Stephanie and her three children are upstairs asleep. After you have set out all of the presents, I'll make some noise to wake them up. Then, when they all come down the stairs, you hand me this little box," Reed said.

I quickly dispersed all of the presents underneath the Christmas tree. I stepped back to make sure everything looked just perfect. Reed stood next to me and admired my work.

"Well done, Kringle."

"Thanks, Reed."

A bright, white light chased across the wall behind the tree. Reed and I spun around and saw a flashlight shining through the front window. We both dropped to the floor behind the ottoman.

"Shhhhhhh, be quiet," I whispered.

The sound of three hard fist-pounds came from the front door.

Reed and I lay on the floor motionless. I looked at him. He looked back at me with a frightened expression.

"No one knows I'm here," Reed whispered.

A hall light turned on upstairs. Three more knocks came from the front door.

"Who is it? I'm coming, I'm coming," a woman said. I turned my head and looked toward the stairs. The woman was coming down the stairs as she tied the robe strap around her waist.

When she got to the bottom of the stairs, she turned on a bright light in the ceiling fan high on the vaulted ceiling. She walked to the front door, turned on the porch light, and looked through the peep hole.

"What is going on?" she said as she opened the door.

Reed and I peered around the ottoman to see who was at the front door.

"It's Stephanie," Reed whispered.

Filling the doorframe were two uniformed county sheriff's deputies. One of them was holding a blinding flashlight pointed at the ground.

"Ma'am, I'm Deputy Cowan, and this is Deputy Drage. We received a call from your neighbors across the street. They reported a suspicious person looking in your front window, and then that person went around the side of your house. May we step in and make sure everyone is safe?"

"Yes, please come in," Stephanie said.

The deputies stepped into the house, and Stephanie closed the door.

From behind the ottoman, Reed said, "Stephanie, it's me, Reed." He slowly stood and put his open palms to his side chest high.

"Reed, what are you doing hiding down there?" Stephanie said with enthusiasm.

"We were delivering some presents," Reed explained.

"We?" Stephanie demanded.

Reed looked down behind the ottoman and motioned for me to stand up. "Yeah, me and . . . Santa," Reed said.

I stood up slowly and assumed the same position as Reed.

"Merry Christmas, Stephanie," I said rather sheepishly. "I was making my Christmas Eve delivery, and Reed asked me to help him deliver his present too," I explained.

Just then, three children dressed in their new Christmas jammies came bouncing down the stairs.

"These are my three children. Maddie is nine, Matt is six, and Robbie is four," Stephanie said to the deputies, pointing at each one as she said their name.

The three kids looked over at Reed and me. Maddie shook her head, and the two boys laughed.

"I have delivered all of your presents and put them under the tree," I said. "But there is one last present Reed wants to deliver." I elbowed Reed.

"All of you come over here in the living room," Reed invited. Stephanie and the children came over to the seating area and sat down on the long couch together.

"We'll just stand here," Deputy Drage said. The deputies remained standing near the couch.

Reed approached Stephanie and the children. He took a small box wrapped in gold paper from his pajama pocket. He knelt in front of Stephanie and the children.

"Maddie, Matt, and Robbie, you know I love you guys with all of my heart. We couldn't be closer if you were my own kids. I'm crazy about all three of you," Reed said.

Stephanie just melted. Tears were forming in her eyes. She gave Reed the most beautiful smile.

Reed bent down on one knee and held the box out in front of the children.

"Maddie, Matt, and Robbie, I'm asking you if I can marry your mom," Reed said.

Maddie's eyes lit up with excitement. Matt and Robbie started bouncing up and down on the couch. Maddie reached out and took the gift from Reed. She looked at Matt and Robbie; they were both nodding yes as they continued to bounce.

"We say yes. Now it's up to Mom," Maddie said. Maddie turned and handed the gift to Stephanie.

"Open it, open it!" Robbie yelled, still bouncing on the couch.

Stephanie took the gift from Maddie and slowly unwrapped it. She dropped the wrapping paper on the floor. Reed slid over in front of Stephanie. Reed took the box, opened it, and presented the ring to Stephanie.

"Stephanie, I love you more than words can express. Every day with you is pure joy. I am a better person when I'm with you. You are my angel, my sweetheart, and my best friend. I want to spend the rest of our lives together and grow old together. Babe, will you marry me?"

Stephanie held out her left hand in front of Reed. They looked at each other. Reed slipped the ring on Stephanie's finger.

"Yes, I will marry you!" Stephanie said. She leaped to her feet and Reed grabbed Stephanie in a big bear hug, picked her off the ground, and swung her back and forth.

Deputies Cowan and Drage began clapping. The kids joined Reed and Stephanie in the big hug. They all held each other tight and giggled. I added to the clapping.

"This is the best Christmas ever," I heard Robbie say from somewhere in the depths of the hug.

When they ended the hug, Stephanie wiped the tears from her eyes with her long pajama sleeve.

"We need to get pictures or else no one is going to believe this happened," I said.

Reed reached over and retrieved his cellphone from the coffee table.

"Men, you need to be in the picture," I said as I gestured for the deputies to go stand by the family.

"Let's do it over here in front of the Christmas tree," Stephanie directed.

The family stood in front of the Christmas tree. Deputy Cowan stood on the left side of them, and Deputy Drage stood on the right side.

"Say 'Rudy,'" I said.

"Rudy!" the family cheered. The deputies gave medium-sized smiles.

"Santa, let me take a picture with you in there," said Deputy Cowan. I jumped in and traded places with him.

"Say 'Comet,'" I said.

"Comet!" we all said together, posing for the picture.

Deputy Cowan handed the phone back to Reed. He showed the pictures to Stephanie as he scrolled through them.

"I can't wait for your watch commander to read your report of this call," I said.

Deputy Drage said, "Yeah, we might have you send us one of the pictures so she'll believe us."

The deputies headed to the front door. Stephanie followed close behind them. She opened the door and said, "Thank you for being out here in the middle of the night away from your own families."

"It's our pleasure, ma'am. This was certainly ... memorable," Deputy Cowan said as he and Deputy Drage walked to their cars.

Stephanie turned around and raised her hands over her head and screamed, "Yeah!" and then did a little high-stepping dance.

"Since everybody is up, what if everybody opens one present

right now if you promise to go to your rooms and not come back down here until 8:00 a.m.," I suggested.

"8:00 a.m.?" all three kids chimed in together.

"Yes, 8:00 a.m., deal?" I spoke.

"Okay, Santa, 8:00 a.m.," the children agreed.

"I have to get going. I'm behind schedule," I said.

I walked to the front door, and the three children followed on my heels.

"We want to see the reindeer," Robbie said.

"Oh, not tonight, please. You go open a present. I gotta hit the friendly skies," I said.

Reed and Stephanie waved from across the room as I closed the door behind me. I could hear the children excited to open their one present of Christmas Eve.

I sprinted to the sleigh, knowing I would have to move faster to stay on schedule. As I climbed out of the neighborhood, I looked down at Stephanie's house. The energy was vibrating at a much higher frequency now than when I'd first sneaked in the back door. It warms my heart to see families become united in love and harmony. Christmas is all about creating priceless, lifetime memories. I was focused on the task at hand to get my deliveries completed, but also in a state of flow prepared for the unexpected.

❧ 12 ❧

He is Christmas

The giving of gifts is not something man invented.
God started the giving spree when He gave a gift beyond words—
the unspeakable gift of His Son.

– Unknown

The glow of the moon illuminated the rooftop and yard around the small, white stucco farmhouse; the house looked like it had not received a fresh coat of paint in decades. The house was tucked behind a row of trees on Pioneer Street in a city called Sandy. I assume it was named after the dirt because the region was formed as a delta from the ancient glaciers that pushed sand and silt out of the large canyon to the east.

I landed behind the house so my reindeer could enjoy a quick snack of tall grass that rose out of the snow like little New York skyscrapers.

I slung the heavy bag of Christmas cheer over my left shoulder and sprinted from the sleigh toward the back porch. Sometimes I have to use the back door of homes that don't have chimneys. As I got closer to the porch, I stopped dead in my tracks. There was a bounty of beautifully wrapped gifts and a number of spectacular presents that didn't need to be wrapped, like a red mountain bike with a big red bow on the handlebars. There were boxes and baskets of food and other assorted household treasures.

Have I already been to this house and forgot to take all of the gifts inside? I thought. *No, impossible.*

I tiptoed up the back stairs and stood in front of the cache of presents. There was a white envelope on top of one of the presents. It was addressed to me. I opened the envelope and read the handwritten note:

Dear Santa:

We know you will be going inside this home to deliver presents tonight. An amazing family that needs a little extra help this year lives here. As you know, the dad lost his job earlier this year, and the mom is working two jobs to make ends meet. The two kids, Rachel and Michael, are the sweetest children, and we want to make their Christmas morning extra special. Our neighborhood pitched in to help us get what this family really needs. It has been a great experience for all of our families to rally behind this family. Will you please take our gifts inside and deliver them with the ones you are delivering from the North Pole? This way our gifts can remain anonymous. Thank you, Santa, for helping us make this Christmas extra special for our entire neighborhood. We love them and want them to have a merry Christmas.

— The Neighborhood Elves

I smiled and chuckled with a soft "ho, ho, ho" under my breath. It warms my heart when I see neighborhoods united to help one another. The strong force of elfishness is alive and well here.

As I cracked the back door open, I was immediately greeted with that special feeling we receive when we resonate with the frequency of the 528 tuning fork. You know immediately when you are in an environment in harmony with that frequency.

I slid my bag from my shoulder and placed it on the faded hardwood floor that covered the entire house. The only light in the room was coming from a tiny Christmas tree; it was only about three feet tall sitting on top of a small, round table with four wooden legs nestled in the corner of the living room. The tree was decorated with a single strand of tiny white bulbs, paper ornaments colored with crayons, popcorn strung together in a simple chain, and a handmade angel adorned the top of the tree. The family who lived here were obviously of very simple means and didn't have much at all. The small living room was sparsely furnished with a well-used couch along one wall below the window with a tattered throw rug in front of it. There was a wingback chair in the other corner.

I dragged my bag along the hardwood floor toward the tree. I unpacked my bag and arranged all of the presents from the North Pole in front of the Christmas tree. I returned to the back porch and made several trips to haul in the gifts from the neighbors. The neighbors were generous and had thought of everything, all kinds of things a family needs for everyday living, plus some fun things for the kids. I was touched by the generosity and caring of the neighbors who had given with so much thought and care.

The presents I delivered combined with the gifts from the neighbors filled the small living room. I knelt down to arrange the last gift; one of my bells rubbed against the pedal on the bike. I froze, gritted my teeth, and cringed, hoping to restrain the echo of the sound from traveling throughout the tiny house. I paused for a moment to listen for any response.

Have you ever had the feeling you know someone is watching you? I gingerly turned my head toward the doorway from the living room to the hallway. I was busted. I was caught in the act of making this delivery. Standing a few feet behind me was a beautiful little girl; it was Rachel, the seven-year-old girl of the family. The reflection of the Christmas lights sparkled in her eyes. Our gazes met, and there was that magical connection I experience when a child looks into my eyes with such wonder, such belief, such love. I pursed my lips, raised my cheeks, and smiled. Rachel was wearing a long night shirt that went down to her ankles. It had a nostalgic holiday print on it. She looked as surprised as I was. She obviously couldn't believe she was standing in front of Santa on Christmas Eve. I rolled back off of my knees and crossed my legs in front of me. I lifted my right index finger to my mouth to communicate silently.

I then motioned for Rachel to come over and sit on my left knee. She tiptoed across the hardwood floor, being so careful not to make any noise. She was just a few feet in front of me when one of the floorboards made a squeak. She stopped mid-step and looked at me with a terrified expression. She took two or three fast steps toward me, leaped, and landed on my knee. We smiled at each other and shrugged. She reached her arms around my neck and gave me a mighty squeeze.

Out of the corner of my eye, I saw Michael, Rachel's little four-year-old brother peeking from behind the door frame. Michael pulled away out of sight and then peeked again. He knew I saw him, so he stepped into the doorway and stared at me. He rubbed his eyes to be more awake. His face was expressionless, and he probably thought he was dreaming. I smiled at him and motioned for him to come to me. I pointed at my right knee. He sauntered over and plopped on my right knee. He leaned in close to my face and looked me in the eye and touched my cheek to discern if I was real. I sensed Mom and Dad were awake now and they were standing in the hall just around the corner. I noticed Mom peek into the room to make sure everything was all right. She disappeared, and I could hear a faint whisper of conversation she was having with Dad. Rachael and Michael looked at each other and then back at me.

I whispered, "Who knows what Christmas is really all about?"

Rachel looked at me and then sprung to her feet. She ran over to the tiny Christmas tree and reached under the bottom row of branches to expose a tiny, plastic nativity scene like you'd find at All-a-Dollar. I hadn't even noticed it when I was arranging all of the gifts. Rachel carefully reached into the stable with two fingers and plucked baby Jesus from the manger. She cupped her other hand under the figurine like a saucer to protect it as she scampered back over to me. She stood right in front of me. She reached out with her empty hand and grabbed my left hand and pulled it in front of her. She carefully placed baby Jesus in the palm of my hand. She then took both of her hands and folded my hand closed.

With the voice of an angel, she whispered, "Santa, He is Christmas."

My heart stopped. The magical frequency surged from my heart out to my fingers and toes. I inhaled and caught my breath.

"Yes, Rachel, He is Christmas."

Michael looked at me, fully aware now that he was not dreaming. I smiled at him, nodded, and repeated, "He is Christmas."

In that moment, it was as though the windows of heaven opened up and pure love flooded the room. There was an abundance of joy that confirmed to me that the world could be healed if we all shared more of the magic Rachel, Michael, and I were sharing.

From the hallway, I could hear Mom and Dad sniffling. They heard Rachel's response to my question. I can only imagine what their hearts were feeling. Their little daughter was sitting on Santa's knee in the middle of the night on Christmas Eve reminding Santa what Christmas is really all about.

I kept baby Jesus clenched in my hand, holding onto the magic of the moment. Tears were welling up in my eyes.

Time stood still. No one blinked.

Rachel, Michael, and I sat together in silence. I looked back at the Christmas tree. The lights were glowing brighter. The room felt warmer.

There are those rare and brief moments in life that leave an indelible mark on our souls; moments we can never duplicate even if we try. Rachel's simple words pierced my soul: "He is Christmas." I was being personally tutored by one of God's little angels to remind me what this magic holiday is really all about.

"Mom and Dad, I know you're in the hall," I said, breaking the silence. "Please come in here and join us."

Mom entered the room first with her hand over her shoulder, holding Dad's hand. I wasn't alone in feeling the sacred nature of this moment. They, too, had eyes full of tears.

Mom and Dad sat on the floor next to us. Michael got up off my knee and went over and sat on his daddy's lap. Dad wrapped his arms around his son, squeezed him tight, and kissed the back of his head.

Mom and Dad both looked around the room, soaking in what was happening. They could see all of the gifts I had delivered from their neighbors. They both looked back at me. Their eyes communicated their gratitude for this special moment.

"Thank you, Santa," Mom said almost inaudibly.

I mouthed the words "You're welcome," because no sound came out of my mouth.

Mom reached over and held Dad's hand.

"Can we sing a song together?" I asked.

"Yes, please," Mom replied.

"There is one song that captures what Christmas is really all about. When I hear this song, I can see the bright star shining brightly over Bethlehem; I can see Joseph, Mary, and the baby Jesus in the stable on that special night when it all began. Go back with me to the early nineteenth century to the small Austrian village of Oberndorf bei Salzburg where this song originates. 'Silent Night,' also known as 'Stille Nacht' in its original German, is one of the most beloved and widely recognized Christmas carols worldwide and my favorite Christmas song."

I began singing, *"Silent night, holy night . . ."*

Mom and Dad joined me, *"All is calm, all is bright . . ."*

Rachel and Michael joined us, *"Round yon Virgin Mother and Child."*

And then I could hear a host in heaven join us,

"Holy infant so tender and mild.

Sleep in heavenly peace.

Sleep in heavenly peace.

Silent night, holy night,

all is calm, all is bright.

Round yon Virgin Mother and Child.

Holy infant so tender and mild.

Sleep in heavenly peace.

Sleep in heavenly peace."

As we sang the last line of the song, I waved my arm like a maestro conducting the heavenly choir to hold the last note. The note echoed into eternity.

"Wow, just wow," Dad said as he exhaled.

"You may forget the presents you receive tonight, but you will never forget the gift, the feeling you have right now in your heart," I said.

Mom wiped tears from her eyes with the back of her hand. She looked at Rachel and Michael like only a mother full of pride for her children could.

"Daddy and I have experienced many special Christmases," she said. "And we can tell you stories about how Christmas was celebrated in our families when both of us were children."

Mom shared a story about large family Christmas gatherings with aunts, uncles, cousins, and grandparents; homemade treats like divinity and fudge while sipping hot cocoa by the fireplace. She talked about reading Bible passages from Luke 2:1–20, describing Jesus' birth to Mary and Joseph—the first Christmas—and singing carols around their own small tree filled with homemade ornaments and paper chains that they'd made themselves.

The nostalgia of those memories had Mom beaming with love even all these years later as if it had just happened yesterday.

Dad then shared a special story that his father had told him about the night of Jesus' birth. "Once upon a time in Bethlehem, it was said by many that on the night of Jesus' birth, a miracle happened—the stars aligned more beautifully than ever before and shone brighter than any other night. In the small town of Bethlehem, shepherds were tending to their flocks when they heard an angel's voice coming from heaven. The angel proclaimed that in Bethlehem, a Savior had been born to all mankind.

"The shepherds raced to find this new baby and followed the star to what would become known as the stable where Christ was born. As they entered, they found only hay and a manger filled with straw—not very grand for such an important event—but there too were heavenly hosts of angels singing praises and showering little newborn Jesus with love and adoration. The shepherds were awe-struck by what they experienced; it was truly something special."

When Dad finished sharing his story, I looked each one of them in the eyes. No more words needed to be spoken.

I lifted Rachel off my lap and stood her up on her feet. I rose to my feet. The rest of the family followed. I stretched out my arms to welcome an embrace. Mom and Dan hugged me as Rachel and Michael hugged them.

"Merry Christmas to this beautiful family, and may God bless you with health and happiness in the new year," I whispered.

"Merry Christmas," they said back to me.

I walked to the door, opened it, and stood in the doorway. I blew them all a kiss on the cheek. They blew me a kiss back. I stepped back out into the crisp night air and pulled the door closed behind me.

As I walked back to my sleigh, I reflected on the tender moments I had just shared with that beautiful family. It was perfect; the neighbors had demonstrated pure elfishness through their service. Rachel had reminded all of us that He is the reason for the season, and we all shared in the magic of the song and stories. My heart was bursting with joy. I didn't want to ever lose that feeling.

I lifted myself onto the sleigh and took hold of the reins. I set off into the velvety blackness of the night sky. The only sounds were the jingling bells of the reindeer and the quiet rustle of the wind rushing past me. It was my favorite part of the job, just me and my sleigh, and the endless stretch of darkness filled with sparkling stars. I looked up and spotted a shooting star. It was rare to see a shooting star during this time of year, so I took it as a sign—a sign that there could be peace on earth if we all lived with the spirit of Christmas every day of the year. I closed my eyes and took a deep breath, letting the cool air fill my lungs.

As I soared through the night sky, I thought about all the people I had visited tonight and throughout the season. All their hopes and dreams, their fears and struggles laid bare before me. I wondered if they knew just how much they had touched my heart and how I was changed by them. My heart was full of gratitude for being blessed to see the world through Santa's eyes.

≈ 13 ≈

Yes, Megan,
There Is a Santa Claus

Christmas Day is in our grasp, as long as we have hands to clasp!
Christmas Day will always be, just as long as we have we!
Welcome Christmas while we stand,
heart to heart, and hand in hand!

– DR. SEUSS

I WALKED INTO MY HOUSE on Christmas morning. Glancing over at the wall in the kitchen, the large clock read 10:45 a.m. I had begun my Christmas Eve Santa appearances at 11:00 a.m. the day before. I was exhausted, but I felt a profound sense of contentment and peace. I had been on an incredible journey over the past few weeks, from immense crowds gathering in joyous celebrations to family gatherings with the warmth of roaring fireplaces, to cozy conversations with kind strangers who shared their stories with me. On this Christmas morning, I felt overwhelmingly blessed.

The house was eerily still, no noises of little feet running down the hall or giggling sounds of happy children. Across the valley was a different scene; Megan and Ben laughing with pure giddiness as they played with their Christmas presents alongside their mom, Lisa. They would spend the morning with her and then I'd pick them up this afternoon for our Christmas Day together.

I went to my bedroom and removed all my Santa gear; I had grown accustomed to wearing it for the nearly sixty events I had appeared in as jolly, old Saint Nick himself.

I laid on my bed to close my eyes for a few minutes to relax and meditate.

"Alexa, play 'Silent Night' by Mannheim Steamroller on repeat," I said. Every time I listen to this rendition of my favorite Christmas song, my spirit soars to a special, heavenly realm.

I closed my eyes. I took a deep breath in through my nose and pushed my stomach out to its capacity, held it for the count of five, and then pushed my breath back out my pursed lips as though I was blowing it out through a straw. I did this ten times until my body synced up to the vibration of the song.

In my mind, I could see how this adventure had begun; Megan running into the kitchen sounding the alarm of what she had discovered in my bedroom and reading the letter from Santa; the process of my personal transformation to look and feel like Santa. I could see all the faces of the people I had seen throughout the season; I could see their eyes looking into mine with such belief and hope. I could see the little girl backstage asking me to make her brother better. I could see wee Sean Murphy receiving the news that his daddy wouldn't be home for Christmas but knowing he was loved. I could see Monica reading the puzzle and receiving her Christmas miracle. I could see Mary opening the music box and the expression on her face as it played "You Are My Sunshine." I could see Candice opening the envelope and knowing she could give her family everything she had in the folder on her phone. I could see Jacob's face the night before he went home to heaven. I could see the Turley family gathered around the firepit and the magic of that moment. I could see Reed swinging Stephanie around in pure joy. I could see Rachel placing baby Jesus in my hand and holding it tight. I could see the faces of the children who accepted the challenge to be more elfish at all the schools, churches, hospitals, shelters, and family parties I visited. I could see the faces of all the grownups who were touched by the spirit of Christmas. I marinated in the most beautiful feeling that accompanied these memories. I wanted this feeling to last forever; if only I could bottle it up and take a dose of this every day. I felt like I was the luckiest man on earth for seeing the world through Santa's eyes.

I reflected on the tuning fork Santa had given me, and how it taught me that love is a divine frequency a person can transmit, and how it can be received by those who have their hearts open to it. I had not been in tune when I received it, but through my journey as Santa, I was now resonating at 528. Sustaining this frequency was now my choice to make every day.

I opened my eyes and faded back into reality. I jumped out of bed, excited to transform the house into a Christmas paradise. I had been away most of the month playing Santa, so I had to transform our home into a winter wonderland in just a few hours. I needed to decorate the tree and organize the presents, bake my mom's cookie recipe, and prepare a yummy side dish to take to my parents' house for family dinner. Lisa had been the one who made our house a warm and inviting home, so I relied on a little Santa magic to get it done myself.

I picked up Megan and Ben from Lisa's. By the looks on their faces, I could tell they'd had a wonderful experience with Lisa on Christmas Eve and Christmas morning.

As I pulled into the garage and stopped, Megan unstrapped herself from the seatbelt and disappeared into the house. I got Ben out of his car seat and wasn't too far behind.

When we entered the living room, Megan was sitting cross-legged in front of the Christmas tree looking at the presents. I put Ben down, and he ran and sat beside her. I walked over and sat on the floor next to Ben.

"Daddy, why are there more presents here under this Christmas tree?" Megan asked. "We had presents from Santa under the tree at Mom's house. And we both know you're Santa."

"I decided to deliver some of the presents for you and Ben to Mom's house and some of them here so I could watch you open them with me," I said.

Megan smiled at my response. For the next hour or so, we opened presents, played with toys and puzzles, and read a couple of the books they received.

"Daddy, what was Christmas Eve like delivering gifts for Santa?" Megan asked.

"It was magical, Megs," I said. "It's hard to describe everything. It happened so fast."

I told Megan and Ben some of the stories from my Christmas Eve adventures. They hung on every word.

Then, Megan got this serious look on her face.

"Daddy, is there really a Santa Claus?"

"Yes, Megan, there is a Santa Claus," I said. "There is more than one Santa Claus. You know he called me to be one of his special helpers this year. He has many helpers around the world. You don't have to dress up like Santa Claus to be Santa Claus. Moms and dads can be Santa. Grandmas and grandpas can be Santa. Teachers, preachers, and friends can be Santa Claus. Being Santa means you are making Christmas special for someone else. You and Ben can be Santas when you do something nice for someone else without expecting anything in return. Being Santa is a feeling in your heart. It's about having a generous spirit and serving with love, and the other person doesn't know who did it."

"So, Santa can be anyone?" Megan asked.

"Yes, anyone can be Santa, Megs," I said. "And do you want to know a secret?"

"Yes, Daddy."

"Santa Claus doesn't have to be just for Christmas. We can be Santa Claus every day of the year."

Megan climbed into my lap and gave me a squeeze around the neck. "I love you, Daddy. Merry Christmas," she said.

Ben leapt to his feet and joined Megan on my lap. I opened my arms wide and engulfed my kids in a hug more meaningful than ever before. While my family might look far from what I dreamed of as a child, I'd been blessed with the greatest gift of all: the love of my children.

~ 14 ~

The Calling Continues

*Seeing is believing, but sometimes the most real things
in the world are the things we can't see.*

– CHRIS VAN ALLSBURG, FROM *POLAR EXPRESS*

I TUCKED BEN INTO BED. I kissed my sweet son on the forehead.
"Goodnight, son. I love you."

I stepped into Megan's room and slid one of her little play chairs next to the bed. I pulled the covers up to her chin.

"Did you have a good Christmas today, Megs?" I asked.

"Yes, Daddy. It was a good Christmas," Megan replied.

"What made it so good?"

"Family time," Megan answered. "I spent time with Mommy and you."

I kissed my beautiful daughter on the cheek.

"Goodnight, Megs, I love you."

"Goodnight, Daddy, I love you too."

I went to my bedroom to get ready for bed and to put a few

things away. I stepped into the walk-in closet and removed a tuxedo from the garment bag it was in. I hung the Santa suit on the hanger and zipped it up. I put the rest of the Santa gear in a tote and placed it on the top shelf of the closet. As I slid the tote back onto the shelf, I saw the phone Santa had given to me with the tuning fork. I hadn't used the phone since early in the season to communicate with Santa. I had been so busy and had forgotten all about it. I pulled the tote down off the shelf and retrieved the phone. I touched the screen, and it illuminated. I pressed the single app displayed in the center of the phone.

"Well, hello there, Coz. I wondered if you were going to call me," Santa said.

"There were a number of times I was going to call you and ask for your advice, but ... I figured you were too busy to take my call," I said.

"Horse hockey," Santa said. "I was never too busy for you. All you had to do was call and I'd be there for you."

"I know, I know," I said. "I don't have any excuses."

"You did it," Santa said. "I was watching you all season. You honored my name and did everything just right. You knew when to be funny. You knew when to be serious. You listened with your heart and had courage to act boldly. Well done. I'm proud of you. Just like Dorothy, the Scarecrow, the Tin Man, and the Lion, you had everything you needed already inside of you. You didn't need me. You just needed to open your heart and let it out."

"Thank you, Santa," I said with a lump growing in my throat. "That was the most magical Christmas adventure I could have ever imagined."

"So, are you done being Santa?" he asked.

"Yes, I was just putting all of your gear away until next year," I replied.

"But you have not completed your calling," Santa said.

"My calling?"

"Yes, your calling. From this day forward, you will be known throughout the world as 'Santa Coz.' I give you full authorization to wear my gear anywhere in the world on any day that ends with a Y," Santa explained.

I chuckled. "Any day that ends with a Y?"

"Yes, any day that ends with a Y, ho, ho, ho. The world needs you, me, and others like us more than ever before. Take our simple 'Be Less Selfish, Be More Elfish' message to every corner of the world. Shout it from every rooftop. Share it with every ear who will hear. Working together, we can change the world and make it a better place for all of us. Can I count on you, Santa Coz?"

"Yes, Santa, you can count on me. I'm all in," I said.

"I know I can count on you. Go make me proud," Santa said.

There was a click, and Santa was gone.

So, my calling continues to take the simple "Be Less Selfish, Be More Elfish" message to the world. I invite you to accept the challenge. Together, we will change the world. May every day of your life be filled with the magic and spirit of Christmas.

PICTURES FROM "THE PUZZLE"

～ 15 ～

Love is the Answer

Thou shalt love the Lord thy God with all thy heart,
and with all thy soul, and with all thy mind.
This is the first and great commandment. And the second
is like unto it, Thou shalt love thy neighbor as thyself.

– HOLY BIBLE, MATTHEW 22:37–39

I HAVE WRITTEN a bonus chapter available for download. Visit **www.ThroughSantasEyes.com** and go to the "Bonus Chapter" link.

Letter to Santas Around the World

To my brothers who serve and have been chosen to wear the sacred red suit, I invite you to join our movement and be an ambassador of love and light.

The world needs you more than ever before. I challenge you to be a powerful agent of global transformation and lead by example. Our simple **"Be Less Selfish and Be More Elfish"** message can change the world. This is more than just a one-time call to action; it's an invitation to embody the spirit of Christmas every day of the year. Imagine the world we would live in if we all lived this way.

Make a commitment to personally **Be More Elfish**. No act of kindness is too small; every conversation, every hug, every smile, and every act of kindness matters.

Rather than asking children what they want for Christmas, ask them what they are going to give for Christmas. Remind them to give gifts from the heart, not just the kind they can order from Amazon or buy in a store. Remind them that Christmas is not about what they get, but what they give. Challenge everyone you meet to **Be More Elfish**.

Help create opportunities for others to **Be More Elfish**. Let's be united and encourage people around the world to love and serve one another. Show them that by joining forces, we can create a more compassionate and caring world.

On your journey as Santa, you will no doubt encounter challenging situations. Remember, it's not about you, it's about those you serve. Find the courage to be kind, generous, and compassionate. Be in tune with the frequency of love and you will attract more of it into your life.

I invite you to share your stories with me at love@throughsantaseyes.com. I'd love to hear about your adventures, experiences, and miracles you witness through Santa's eyes.

Thank you for being a part of the movement. May your journey be filled with love, compassion, and joy.

Warm regards,

Santa Coz

ACKNOWLEDGMENTS

I ACKNOWLEDGE and am deeply grateful to all the powers and people who have been a part of this journey to make *Through Santa's Eyes* a reality.

First, I thank God, my Creator, the Divine, for blessing me with the inspiration and ability to transcribe the words dictated to me. I'm grateful for the talents and abilities leased to me during my mission on Earth to bless and inspire the lives of countless people around the world.

I'm grateful for my children, Megan and Ben, for holding such a special place in my heart and for being my North Star. My relationship with them is my greatest gift in life. I cherish each moment we share together. I'm grateful for Megan's husband, Dennis, and my beautiful granddaughter Aurora "Rory." You will learn more about my amazing children in this book.

I'm grateful for my parents, Paul and Delpha, for doing their best to raise me. I'm grateful for my mother who sacrificed dearly for me to explore my natural gifts and find my unique place in the world. I'm grateful for my brother, Kelvin, and sister, Paulanne, their families, and my extended family for all they have done throughout my life.

I'm grateful for my "little brother" Mark Simpson. He is not my biological brother, but we couldn't be closer. We've shared so many priceless experiences together in the past fifty years. I'm grateful for Mark's love and support to make our movement possible.

I'm grateful to Lisa Green for blessing me with two amazing children. She is the best mother our children could ever have.

I'm grateful for all the people whose stories I share in this book. You changed my life as I witnessed your love through Santa's eyes.

I'm grateful for Ginger Rawson for being a special angel in my life.

I'm grateful for the Haws family who made me feel special and loved in their home; and for all the families and friends who touched my life growing up in Midvale, Utah.

I'm grateful for Dick Reep for truly seeing me and helping a shy, introverted kid blossom into the entertainer I became.

I'm grateful for Paul Earnshaw who gave me my first job in radio and mentored me as a young news reporter.

I'm grateful for Don Gull for all his faith and support throughout all my unique experiences in Northern Ireland and the Republic of Ireland.

I'm grateful for Brian Tracy and the dramatic influence he had in my early twenties and for developing me as a speaker, trainer, and coach.

I'm grateful to Dennis Pennington for believing in this book and consistently kicking my butt to finish it.

I'm grateful for Rob Diamond who gave me the title for this book and encouraged me to tell these stories.

I'm grateful to Richard Paul Evans, the author of The Christmas Box, for his influence on this book. He is the Godfather of Christmas books.

I'm grateful for all my friends around the world who have influenced my life and shaped my soul. You know who you are. I'm grateful for all my associates I've worked with in entertainment, broadcasting, media, and sports.

I'm grateful to you for reading this book. I hope you will feel the same joy and appreciation for this message as I do. I hope it will touch your heart and encourage you to live each day with the true spirit of Christmas and **Be More Elfish**. Together, we can make the world a better place. May you be blessed in your journey.

QUIET GIVING

About the Author

Coz Green began as a professional, award-winning entertainer at the age of 13 and continues to perform around the world.

Coz started his broadcasting career as a news reporter for an ABC talk radio station at the age of 17. His success in broadcasting and media spans over three decades. He is a major league sports announcer, and his voice can be heard nationally on numerous voice-over projects.

As an international speaker, Coz inspires audiences on a variety of business and personal development topics. He champions charity causes and raises millions of dollars as a producer, emcee, and auctioneer.

Coz is the proud father of two amazing children, Megan and Ben, and pappy to a beautiful granddaughter Aurora "Rory."

Visit **www.CozGreen.com** for more information.

For each copy sold of *Through Santa's Eyes*, a portion will be donated to **The Christmas Box House International**, US 501(c)(3) Nonprofit.

The Christmas Box House International's mission is inspired by the spirit and message of The Christmas Box, a book that emphasizes the beauty and importance of love for children.

The Christmas Box International partners with local, national, and international communities and groups to prevent child abuse and improve the quality of life for children, teens, and young adults who have been abused, neglected, or faced homelessness.

The Christmas Box International has selected the following primary areas of focus to accomplish its mission:

1. Collaborate in the development of temporary shelter and assessment centers for children that are abused, neglected, or abandoned.

2. Assist older youth as they transition out of foster care into adult living.

3. Advocate for the provision of the highest quality of care and services to at-risk children.

4. Promote partnerships among government agencies, charitable organizations, the business community, and compassionate community members to provide optimal care and support to the children.

5. Develop international partners to assist children worldwide.

For more information and to donate, visit their website: TheChristmasBox.org

Thank you for your love and support.

Coming in 2024